ED. Matadores
Revolutionizing the Educational System

Donna Vallese, PhD, Founder of Inspiring Leaders
María Angélica Benavides, EdD, B-Global Publisher
Dr. Randi Ward, Editor

Donna Vallese, PhD • María Angélica Benavides, EdD • Randi D. Ward
Dr. Beverly Knox-Pipes • Casanova Green • Cindy Buckner Starke, MD, PhD
Cynthia Bruton-Thomas • Eliezer Hernández, Ed.D • Dr. Emily R. Van Dyke
Erum Manzoor • Dr. Heinrich Heinrichs • Dr. Jerri-Lynn Williams-Harper
Ioanna Mantzouridou Onasi • Joe Griffin, PhD • Kai Smith, Ph.D
Kevin Wayne Johnson • Louise Debreczeny, Ed.D. • Dr. Maria Rodriguez
Mary L. Jones • Maryjane Sander M.Ed. • Sam Aquino Drohin • Tadios Belay
Timothy Andrew Smith, EdD • Trish Persen MEd, MFA

ED. Matadores

ED. Matadores
Revolutionizing the Educational System

Published by B-Global Publishing.
Copyright © 2023

ISBN: 979-8-9887303-2-3

All rights reserved. No part of this book may be reproduced, distributed, or transmitted in any form or by any means, electronically or mechanically, including photocopying, recording, information storage, and retrieval systems, without the prior written permission of the publisher, except in the case of brief quotations embodied in critical reviews and specific other noncommercial uses permitted by copyright law. For permission requests, write to the publisher, addressed "Permission Request" at support_staff@drbglobal.net

This book may be purchased for educational, business, or promotional sales. Special discounts are available on quantities corporations, associations, and others purchase. For more information or to order additional copies of this book, contact the publisher at the address above.

Orders by U.S. trade bookstores and wholesalers.
Email support_staff@drbglobal.net

B-Global Publishing brings authors to your live event. For more information or to book an event, contact support_staff@drbglobal.net

All information written in this book is written solely for motivation and direction. No financial guarantees. All information is considered valid and factual to the authors' knowledge. The authors are affiliated with the companies mentioned in their bio's. The authors are not associated with a brief mention of other companies or brands mentioned in the book and do not purposefully advertise or receive payment from any company.

The authors and publisher do not assume and hereby disclaim any liability to any party for any loss, damage, or disruption caused by errors or omissions.

Manufactured and printed in the United States of America and distributed globally by B-Global Publishing

Table Of Contents

Dedication	1
Foreword	2
Acknowledgements	3
Introduction *Ed. Matadores: Catalyst of Educational Revolution*	4

LEADERSHIP

Leadership Without Moral Courage Does Not Exist By Eliezer Hernández	9
Leadership Is Essential By Kevin Wayne Johnson	17
Lead Toward Change By Dr. Beverly Knox-Pipes	22
Leadership and Change Management for Public School Entities By Dr. Jerri-Lynn Williams-Harper	31

GIVING A VOICE

Beyond Labels: Nurturing Creative Voices, Inspiring Youthpreneurship, And Transforming Education By María Angélica Benavides	39
Give Everyone A Voice By Dr. Maria Rodriguez	48
Recognizing The Power Of Collective Communication: Taming The Stubborn Bull And Unveiling The Big Why In Education By Trish Persen	57

SERVING THE UNDERSERVED

Still Facing The Same Problems By Kai Smith	66
Empowering Girls In STEM Education: A Revolution In Progress By Erum Manzoor	73
SHATTERED FOUNDATIONS Linked to Youth Homelessness. TRUTHS // Youths, Financial Literacy, And Homelessness By Mary L. Jones	80

Confronting The High School Academic Arms Race & Confronting The Potential Chilling Effect On College Campus Diversity In The Post-Affirmative Action Era By Dr. Emily R. Van Dyke — 87

Leveling The Playing Field: An Introduction To Justice Pedagogy By Casanova Green — 94

INTERNATIONAL EDUCATION

Promoting Diversity And Fostering Belonging: The Role Of Virtual Exchange To Support Historically Marginalized Students In U.S. Higher Education By Dr. Tadios Belay — 102

Filling The Social Gap With H3 - Head, Hand, And Heart: Competency Based Vocational Training The Africrops! Way By Dr. Heinrich Heinrichs — 110

NEUROSEMANTICS

Drawing: The Eighth Literacy By Louise Debreczeny, Ed.D. — 118

Using A Visual Teaching Method By Maryjane Sander — 126

SOCIAL EMOTIONAL LEARNING & DIVERSITY, EQUITY, AND INCLUSION

Bridging The Gap: Modernizing Education For Today And Tomorrow By Sam Aquino Drohin — 134

DIPP Approach Framework For Future Success By Dr. Joe Griffin — 142

Empowering Educators: Nurturing The Seeds Of Personal Growth By Unveiling Blind Spots In Your Subconscious Mind By Dr. Cindy Starke — 150

Empowering Futures: My CTE-DEI Educational Mission By Cynthia E. Bruton-Thomas — 158

EQUITABLE SCHOOL MODELS

Competency-Based Grading For Equitable Learning By Dr. Donna Vallese — 167

Bridging The Achievement Gap With An Innovative Blended Learning Model By Timothy Andrew Smith — 175

Redefining Education For The Future: The Power Of Soft Skills 183
By Ioanna Mantzouridou Onasi

Conclusion 190

References 193

ED. Matadores

Dedication

We dedicate this book to the resilient students who faced adversity in education and defied a system that didn't always understand them and to students who felt school was not for them, who slipped through the cracks or made it through by the skin of their teeth... Your schooling is only part of your journey, and it does not define you.

This is for the educators whose voices are unheard and the leaders who embrace challenges while advocating for meaningful change, and for the educators who continue doing what is right when your district, state, or government tells you it isn't possible or tells you that you can't... Keep fighting for equity!

We also dedicate this book to the unwavering supporters who believed in us, casting a steady light on our paths even when we doubt ourselves. To those who ignited a spark, guiding us through the shadows and encouraging us to persevere in our journey, no matter the challenges, we are forever grateful. To our closest colleagues, mentors, and thought partners who have inspired us over the years to work outside the box that policies and systems try to keep us neatly working within, keep encouraging others to do this. Your belief and support have been the fuel for our resilience and determination.

May this book inspire a journey beyond the confines of traditional schooling, recognizing that it's only one part of a diverse and dynamic path.

Foreword

Every single day, the challenges of global education become more daunting and more urgent. The poorest children and those living in remote regions have been hit the hardest, but many other children are suffering as well. Our educational programs have become outdated to meet the needs of the 21st century student. We are at a critical inflection point with hundreds of millions of children likely to miss out on a quality education at the very moment where we must also confront climate change, increasing global conflicts, and continuous pandemic risks.

The educational leaders in this Ed. Matadores' book agrees that something different and transformational needs to happen now. But what does transformation mean, anyway? The renowned and highly respected Co-Authors in this incredible anthology share their powerful insights on educational reforms they have used successfully and the innovative programs they have created which have shown positive results with the students in their school systems.

As a retired 37+ year American and International Educator and the Editor of this book, I am highly impressed with the passion and lifetime work being done by these fellow educators. Many more forward-thinking educators like these Co-Authors are essential if the educational needs of our present and future students at all levels from pre-kindergarten classes through university courses are fulfilled to guarantee students the prosperous futures they deserve. The diversity of educational programs discussed in this book are phenomenal, and these diverse programs are impacting education already for minorities, special needs students, and the general student population.

Teachers, parents, and students, this book will inspire you and give you hope that progressive educational reforms are being created and will increase if you become educational activists and demand changes from your school systems. You may want to start by trying to implement some of these programs in your schools.

It takes a "village" to make real changes. Be an active member of your "village".

Ambassador Dr. Randi D. Ward, Lifetime Educator, Former Owner of two Egyptian English Centers, Best-Selling Author/Speaker, Visionary Book Coach/Master Editor, Chancellor of World University of Leadership and Management, Co-Owner of RM Infinite (OneStop Possibilities), Humanitarian

Acknowledgments

A heartfelt thank you to all of the co-authors collaborating in our book series and those who will join, embracing the purpose, mission, and vision of our collective work. Your belief in the power of uniting educational innovators signifies a shared commitment to impact change and revolutionize the educational system. Together, we stand poised to create a transformative ripple in the education landscape.

Special gratitude to Gavin Landless for his valuable assistance in editing and for his support for our ambitious endeavor. Together, we strive to leave the world better than we found, fueled by our collective efforts and dedication to a brighter future.

Special acknowledgement to Dr. Randi D. Ward, whose dedicated collaboration with Dr. B. in editing and crafting the chapters. Dr. Randi has added a spark of light and excellence to every chapter. Her tireless efforts illuminate the voices of these incredible authors, contributing to a work that strives to resonate and inspire in the broader world.

In profound appreciation, we extend our thanks to Shelly Yorgesen for creating the space and opportunities that allowed Dr. Donna and Dr. B. to connect in such an inspiring place... Crom Castle is where this powerful collaboration started, and we will always be grateful for that!

Finally, our heartfelt gratitude goes to the Education 2.0 Conference for providing a consistent space for thought leaders and innovators across multiple fields to unite. This conference allowed us to meet many of the incredible authors of this book and start our journey to revolutionize the educational system in a way that has not been tried before.

Ed. Matadores: Catalyst of Educational Revolution
By Dr. Donna Vallese

Our educational system has scarcely changed in over 150 years, despite our society changing more rapidly than ever. Students still come to school, often sit in rows, listen to lectures, and try hard to pass high-stakes tests. Yet, we have over a century of research that tells us that this is not how children or adults learn best, and it has been proven time and time again. This type of schooling was needed during a time when we were starting production lines during the industrial age... but we are now in a technological and information age. Our needs in a globalized society have changed dramatically, not just in the last century but even more so in the last decade. Schools have not come close to keeping up.

Now with the open access to artificial intelligence (AI) technology, changes are happening at a much more furious pace - faster than the entrance of the personal computer (PC), the Internet, and email. If our schools do not take significant steps to ensure our students are graduating with the necessary skills to be successful in this new world, they will be at a severe disadvantage.

We know that there are innovative models and practices happening. However, they are far and few between. They are happening in some classrooms, in some schools, and in some districts. If you took the world map and dropped a handful of sprinkles over it, where each sprinkle landed would be a good representation of how innovation is happening... very randomly.

Everyone is doing something different to try to meet student needs while attempting to avoid the major roadblocks put up by endless unfunded mandates imposed by lawmakers who know very little about teaching and learning. In addition, short-sighted regulations by departments of education keep us stuck to old Carnegie units of seat time and other outdated practices that suppress true innovation and promote reinventing old models while giving them new names. All of this continues to contribute to a widening achievement gap.

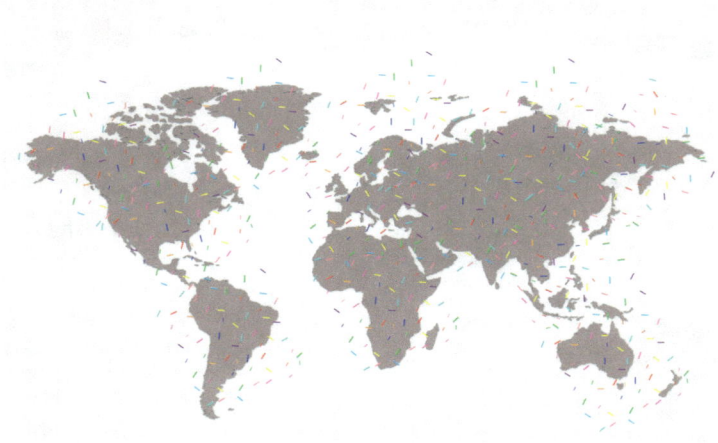

When Dr. Angelica Benevides, a retired Special Education Director, turned publisher, and I met her at Crom Castle in Northern Ireland in April of 2022, we connected right away as education experts with serious concerns about the inequities and inadequacies of our educational system. We knew we needed to collaborate. Over conference calls between New York and Texas, we spent many hours discussing the multitude of failed attempts we had witnessed to try to fix education. We also discussed the innovative change-making differences that we had seen in numerous places. But none of them seemed to have a big impact on systemic change.

As we brainstormed and problem-solved, we reflected on our experiences in professional networking with Executive Networking Events that had brought us together as business owners in a castle of all places. There was something to this networking, creating a synergy between people who cared about making the world better. It was in this reflection that Ed. Matadores was born.

What if we brought together all of the innovative leaders in the educational space, told their transformative narratives in a series of books, and built a collective of people who truly were on a mission to revolutionize the entire educational system? If we could build a collective of hundreds or thousands of people we would have our own army of changemakers for a grassroots movement.

Education is likely the second largest system in the world, behind only healthcare. It is a vast system with deep roots. While all of these amazing innovations are happening on the surface, we really need something that will start to address the root causes of ineffective practices and policies in the multiple layers of the educational system.

Some people have asked how we chose our title, Ed. Matadores. On the surface, we are educational (or Ed.) innovators who are trying to end the roadblocks (or the bulls) that are getting in the way of progress and creating unnecessary inequities for our children. In my activist street band, UNiTY Street Band, we play a tune called Matador by Los Fabulosos Cadillacs. It is a song of resistance from Argentina, told from the point of view of a revolutionary they called "El Matador." A section of the Spanish lyrics translate to English as:

> "I don't have to be afraid, my words are bullets
> Peace bullets, justice bullets
> I am the voice of those who got silenced for no reason
> By the mere fact of thinking differently."

ED. Matadores

Every day, every month, and every year seems to fly by. Change seems hard to make while you are flying the plane of education, but each day that passes is time that our children do not get back. The work of revolutionizing the entire educational system so that it meets the needs of current society is urgent. Whether you are a parent, a student, a relative, a policy maker or a lawmaker, an educator, an employer, or anyone else who has a stake in ensuring that our children are served in ways that allow their brilliance to develop and shine, we invite you to join us on this journey to change the educational system.

The time is now.

ED. Matadores

LEADERSHIP

Eliezer Hernández, Ed.D.
Educational Leader

Eliezer Hernández, Ed.D. is a career educator with 25+ years of professional and community involvement. His experience as a teacher, principal, coach, district leader, and school board member spans from suburban to urban school districts. Dr. Hernández has held executive leadership roles in small and mid-sized non-profit, civil rights, and social justice organizations. He is the Founder of Authentic LeaderShift, LLC, a certified Maxwell Leadership Team Member, Facilitator, Speaker, Trainer, and DISC Behavioral Consultant on personal, professional, and organizational growth and development.

Leadership Without Moral Courage Does Not Exist
By Eliezer Hernández, Ed.D.

Creating high-achieving schools begins with educational leaders having the moral courage to act regardless of the consequences. School leaders are expected to provide a safe and productive environment while ensuring students have an appropriate education. In addition to navigating historical challenges in antiquated educational systems, leaders are required to manage adults' attitudes and behaviors that impact student achievement. Leaders' decisions are widely influenced by their life history, shaping their values, beliefs, and attitudes (Guerra et al., 2016). In professional practice, personal beliefs are a greater predictor of a person's behavior than professional knowledge (Nelson & Guerra, 2014). So, how do social justice-minded school leaders challenge both their personal beliefs and the structures, cultures, and policies that deny students equitable opportunities for success (Shields, 2017)?

Experiencing School as a Bilingual Student

Growing up in a bilingual, single-parent household in the South Bronx, I learned that the most effective form of assisting others is through education. When my family arrived in New York, our mother had to work several jobs to support her four children. When we registered in the NYC public school system, at first, we each attended different schools. One of our principals was bilingual and could communicate with my mother. After a meeting with that principal, we were provided the necessary resources to be academically successful, which included access to full transportation, free meals at school, and the ability to attend the same school. Had the communication with a bilingual administrator not taken place, my mother would not have had knowledge of these available resources for her children.

My experiences as a Hispanic student taught me about educators' and school leaders' attitudes, behaviors, and hidden beliefs. Educators have both the power to make students feel optimistic and the power to discourage them. The negative high school experiences I endured could have derailed my path. Fortunately, my strong faith and family-based foundation propelled me to overcome many challenges. At the same time, other educators' attitudes, behaviors, and beliefs reinforced my confidence in achieving anything.

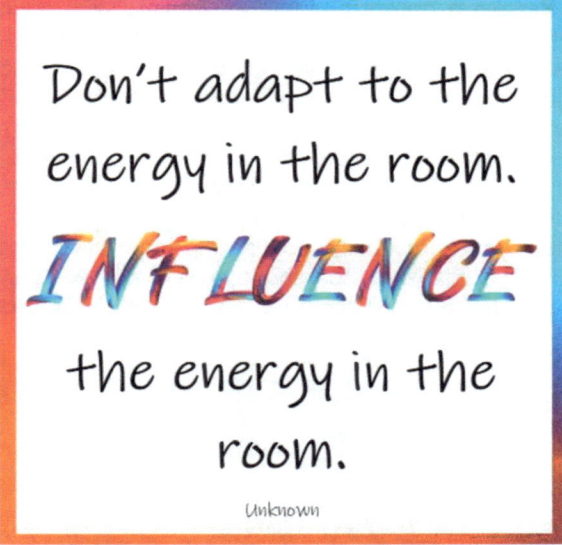

Encountering Roadblocks to Social Justice as a Professional

Ten years later, when I became a Spanish teacher at a high school, I realized that regardless of the expectations set on teachers to remain neutral when teaching, some educators did not. Some of my students shared their experiences in their history classes with me. Teachers taught the students history based on their personal and political views and beliefs, which resulted in the students developing their beliefs based on the information the teachers provided. Students were protective of what they learned in class and had difficulty accepting different views. The failure of teachers to present all sides of history was disheartening. As a result, students were unequipped to form their own unbiased conclusions.

My lived experiences of persistence and perseverance led me to become a school leader. I wanted to impact students, primarily black and brown children, who needed to see a reflection of themselves. As a school leader, I thought I was going to help students. However, my actual job was leading adults, which proved incredibly complex. As a middle school vice principal in an urban school district, I learned that the adults held strong personal beliefs, often hindering student progress. Fortunately, our principal believed all students could achieve; therefore, he often challenged the staff with opposing beliefs. Shifting the mindsets and beliefs of adults is difficult work.

It is crucial to take a hard stance when dealing with social justice and equity for all students. Kouzes and Posner (2012) assert that becoming an exemplary leader requires grasping the deeply held values—the beliefs, standards, ethics, and ideals—that drive you (p. 48). Leadership is not about charisma but behavior (Kouzes & Posner). Educational leaders' influences and beliefs are essential to school reform and classroom outcomes (DeMatthews & Mawhinney, 2014; Leithwood et al., 2004). Social justice leadership requires school leaders to "make issues of race, class, gender, disability, sexual orientation, and other historically and currently marginalizing conditions in the United States central to their advocacy, leadership practice, and vision" (Theoharis, 2007, p. 223).

As evident in DeMatthews and Mawhinney's (2014) study of two principals leading for social justice, these school leaders attempted to create an inclusive environment for all students by eliminating segregated classrooms of special education students with disabilities. However, an increase in negative student behaviors inhibited these inclusionary practices. Consequently, the principals reverted to pulling students out of the inclusive classrooms to provide individual instruction. This pullout model denies students access to the classroom curriculum and creates marginalized groups within an already marginalized group. However, DeMatthews (2015) highlights an urban elementary school principal's ability to create a more inclusive school, resulting in a different outcome. When faced with behavioral challenges similar to DeMatthews and Mawhinney's (2014) study, the school leader created a discipline committee comprised of teachers that focused on identifying students who needed behavioral support. The committee developed an intervention matrix with all the school's social, emotional, and behavioral services. Including teachers in the committee ensured their buy-in to the process, which assisted in building staff capacity, creating structures that supported all students, and addressing the deficit perspectives of staff and teachers.

Demonstrating Moral Courage

To gain commitment from constituents, morally courageous leaders must model desired behaviors for others to emulate in the workplace. Northouse (2018) asserts that the "process whereby a person engages with others and creates a connection that raises the level of motivation and morality in both the leader and the follower is transformational leadership" (p. 162). I conducted a study to understand how high-achieving urban school leaders' beliefs were influenced by their lived experiences and how their beliefs were reflected in their leadership practices. When their beliefs met disorienting dilemmas, the school leaders found themselves navigating through uncharted territories. After a self-examination and a critical assessment of their assumptions, these school leaders were able to acquire new knowledge and skills, plan a course of action, and implement a plan. As a result, they were able to close the achievement gap in their schools successfully.

After becoming a turnaround principal in 2014, I led a bilingual school in an urban district with an 87% poverty rate. Like the school leaders in the study, I experienced a disorienting dilemma when leading two schools simultaneously. After several attempts to improve assessment scores, the state phased out one school, and a bilingual program began in the phase-in school. Despite high discipline, behavioral concerns, deficit mindsets, a demoralized staff, students, and community members, and grieving the loss of two influential staff members, we addressed school behavior through universal intervention, celebrated instructional wins, and attended to faculty needs. By doing so, our students were able to learn and gain confidence again. The school phased out, meeting most of the receivership indicators. At the same time, a state shortage of bilingual teachers plagued our phase-in bilingual school. Throughout the years, we worked hard to secure bilingual educators; we challenged the district to learn more about the benefits of bilingual education, collaborated with higher learning institutions to create cohort models of bilingual educators at reduced tuition rates, and continued developing innovative teaching methods for our students.

The following school leaders' vignettes show real-life examples demonstrating moral courage:

Vignette 1: A first-year principal described her elementary school as dirty, with graffiti all over the school hallways and multiple layers of cracked paint. Many of the classrooms had dim and flickering lighting. After following the district procedures and going as high up the chain of command as possible, her request to paint her building was denied as it was on the list for repainting in several years. Understanding the depressing physical conditions of her school, she defied district policy and, with a few dedicated friends and educators, transformed the building before the start of the school year. However, that was not enough. After receiving a standing ovation from parents, students, and faculty on the first day of school, she stood in front of the staff and asked them "why" they allowed the conditions of the building to go for so long. From that moment forward, she empowered her staff to be champions for their students and families.

Vignette 2: A principal in a dual language school fought to provide the students with an equitable education by advocating for a robust Spanish Language Arts curriculum. This principal also challenged the mindsets of the staff and the district on the dual language students' ability to be successful on the English Language Arts (ELA) state assessments. As a result of implementing the Spanish Language Arts curriculum, the school's proficiency on the ELA assessments increased from 2% to 15% in four years.

Vignette 3: One principal strategically changed instruction to meet the needs of all her students. Her defiance and bold decisions met resistance from the district. After showing significant growth in the ELA assessments, the district attempted to systematize the changes districtwide. They were unsuccessful. Every school is unique and must receive what it needs.

Vignette 4: A high school principal implemented intentional Professional Learning Communities for her veteran staff. She also made critical changes in the master schedule by shifting the core essential courses needed for graduation to earlier in the day. As a result, the graduation rate jumped from 28% to 93% in one year. Despite the scores being questioned by the district, the school proved that urban schools could excel when deficit mindsets changed.

Revolutionizing the System for Social Justice

Moral courage is the willingness to take a stand that may require extreme emotional or social discomfort, tolerate tension, and engage in activism and advocacy (Shield, 2010). Despite the systemic structures that continue to impact urban schools negatively, school leaders must find unique ways to make the necessary changes that support student growth and achievement. Overall, school leaders must exhibit the moral courage to dismantle all unjust systems that hinder progress in urban schools. If this is the case, what measures should school leaders with moral courage take to close the achievement gap once and for all?

One way to start is by continuing to inspire school leaders to do what is right for students and families and not worry about the political fallout of leading a school. School leaders must be multifaceted and versatile enough to handle all aspects of the educational environment. Morally courageous leaders distribute leadership, are unafraid to start from the ground up, lead by example, maintain integrity, and take critical action for social justice. Most importantly, school leaders must challenge their assumptions and lead with moral courage (Shields, 2014). In order to revolutionize schools, moral leaders must:
- Transform internal and external biases of self and others into a greater understanding of student needs.
- Develop and share the vision of a socially just school system.
- Build authentic relationships that support the exchange of beliefs and ideas among staff and stakeholders to foster common goals.

School leaders worldwide can change the systemic educational culture in their districts by remaining steadfast in their core values, being willing to face complex challenges, and having the endurance to do what is right.

Enjoy This LeaderShift Gift

Personal development is a lifelong pursuit to better yourself through new experiences, education, and more. Whether you want to achieve personal goals, advance in your career, improve your strengths, or continue improving yourself, personal development is the answer. Now is the perfect time to expand your horizons through personal growth. Take advantage of this Free Personal Development Newsletter, and let's grow together.

Contact Eliezer Hernández, Ed.D.

ED. Matadores

Kevin Wayne Johnson
Founder & Chief Executive Officer
The Johnson Leadership Group LLC

As the Chief Executive of The Johnson Leadership Group LLC, Kevin provides organizations and the people who work within them with the tools to forge effective personnel and interpersonal communication. He delivers training in the elements of dynamic relationships to equip teams with the attitudes and attributes needed to develop individuals into leaders. He is a Maxwell Leadership Team certified trainer, coach, mentor, and speaker, and an active member of the International Coaching Federation. A native of Richmond, Virginia, Kevin is a graduate of Virginia Commonwealth University. Since 2001, he has authored 20 books on diverse topics that have earned 31 literary awards. He has been married to Gail for 30 years; they live in Clarksville, Maryland, and from their union, they have raised three sons.

Leadership Is Essential
By Kevin Wayne Johnson

I learned the qualities and attributes of good leadership at home as the eldest son of a United States Marine Corps officer. Through observation and experience, I gained insight on how and why meaningful and effective leadership can have a positive impact. As a young child who helped to raise my mentally challenged brother and then as a young father who raised an autistic son, I discovered that their differences required my attention to demonstrate empathy, compassion, respect, care, and value. To this end, I found myself asking, *"How can I make this world a better place?"* My answer led me to a career as a teacher, trainer, coach, and mentor and to share with others that how we treat others can be more impactful than what we know. I firmly believe that Ed Matadore's mission of revolutionizing the educational system echoes the same sentiment.

Good leadership is more than a dream. It is a necessity in the home, in the workplace, in our social and civic organizations, in our churches, and in the multiple other venues where leaders use their influence to make a positive impact in the lives of others.

Statistical Findings
Did you know?

Employees at all levels in the workplace feel undervalued, marginalized, and underappreciated in more ways than one. U.S. companies spent $160 billion on employee training and education, yet:
- Fifty-eight percent of managers said they did not receive any *management training*.
- Seventy-nine percent of people quit their jobs due to *lack of appreciation*.
- Seventy-seven percent of organizations report they are currently experiencing a *leadership gap*.
- Only 10% of CEOs believe their company's leadership development initiatives have a *clear business impact*.
- Sixty-three percent of Millennials said their leadership skills were not being *fully developed*.

To address this dilemma, following my retirement from the federal government after thirty-four years as a frontline, mid-level, and senior-level leader in 2017, I founded The Johnson Leadership Group LLC, one year later, whose mission is: *To create leaders of excellence at all levels*. My team of ten diverse professionals and I provide leadership development training, executive coaching, assessment tools, online courses, and diversity-equity-inclusion training and consultation to government agencies, corporations, churches, nonprofit organizations, and academic institutions. Companies around the world are facing a leadership crisis, according to the quarterly report of the 2021 Global Leadership Forecast that was released on May 12, 2021. Only 11% of surveyed organizations reported they have a "strong" or "very strong" leadership bench, the lowest it has been in the past ten years. The crisis can be traced to a failure by companies to provide leadership development and transition training for newly hired and current executives, according to Development Dimensions International (DDI), which conducts the annual survey.

The highest global average rating for bench strength was 18% in 2011. It has been on the decline ever since. The DDI survey was conducted between February 2020 and July 2020. It includes data from more than 15,000 leaders and 2,100 human resource professionals who represent 1,740 organizations in 24 industries globally. Other major findings from the survey include:
- Twenty-eight percent of organizations with high-quality development had a strong leadership bench. Combining assessment tools with development delivered even higher bench strength. On average, combining high-quality assessment with

any development program boosts bench strength by 30%.
- Nearly 40% of organizations with both high-quality development and assessment tools had a strong bench of leaders ready for critical roles.
- Stress wrecks leaders' confidence levels. Nearly half of leaders with stressful transitions rated themselves as average to below-average leaders. One in 16 C-level executives said their transitions were so stressful they often thought about quitting.

Johnson Leadership For Change of Heart

Now 63 years old, I see evidence every day that I am on the right track in leading The Johnson Leadership Group LLC. On more than one occasion, I've witnessed men and women weep publicly during classes as they discussed what they'd learned and how they would apply the new leadership principles and strategies that were taught. It's the result of their change of heart and new way of thinking. They have a renewed focus on how to lead their people and create an environment that is conducive to high performance and improved productivity because they learn about all:
- Empathy.
- Effective communication,
- Compassion, and
- Care for others.

These core behaviors, attributes, mannerisms, and characteristics should be taught in the local church, but most Americans do not attend. They should be taught in the workplace to stop the revolving doors as evidenced by workers leaving their jobs in unprecedented numbers. They should be taught in our academic institutions so that our students, the next generation of leaders, can witness good leadership in action. They should be taught in corporations to shift the never-ending push to generate revenue as a priority over the basic needs of the employees. A key takeaway is to become relational and not dictatorial in their approach to leadership. Additionally, the Small Business Administration and other Fortune 500 companies provided access to emergency funding during COVID-19 to sustain day-to-day small business operations throughout the U.S.A. This includes the Payroll Protection Program, the Economic Injury Disaster Loan, and business grants of various amounts. While I did hear about the many miscues and missteps regarding the rollout of these programs, I personally experienced little to no concerns. My business was approved for every source of funding that I applied for except one. The one $10,000 grant request that I did not receive was due to my own error in misreading the instructions and guidelines. The funding has assisted The Johnson Leadership Group LLC in our recurring pursuit to support our myriad of clients in the marketplace without a hiccup while continuing to build the business daily and grow internationally.

I believe that leaders are learners. Our thirst should never be quenched, and our hunger should never be satisfied when it comes to serving others in a leadership capacity. Better leaders help to make the world a much better place.

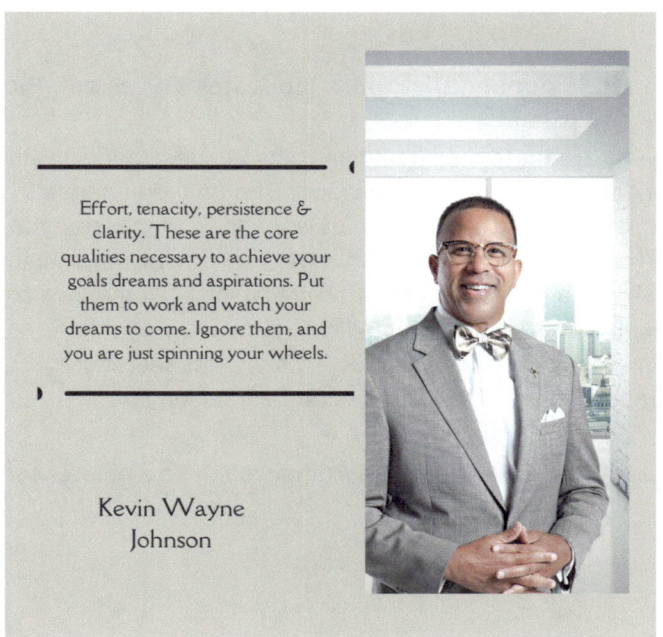

Effort, tenacity, persistence & clarity. These are the core qualities necessary to achieve your goals dreams and aspirations. Put them to work and watch your dreams to come. Ignore them, and you are just spinning your wheels.

Kevin Wayne Johnson

Dr. Beverly Knox-Pipes
Founder/CEO/Senior Consultant
BKP Solutions

Leader. Visionary. Disruptor. Innovator. Strategist. Pioneer

Dr. Beverly Knox-Pipes embodies these descriptors with passion, commitment, and fierce determination. She has led change in education for over 40 years through her outspoken and passionate advocacy balanced with her down-to-earth style. As an award-winning thought leader, she is a sought-after speaker/advisor at numerous conferences and organizations, most recently as the invited Keynote speaker at the Education 2.0 conference. Dr. Beverly's vibrant and courageous voice is transformative in both the business and education space:

"Be Courageous! Be Curious! Be Authentic! Make a difference!"

Lead Toward Change
By Dr. Beverly Knox-Pipes

"In times of change, learners inherit the earth; while the learned find themselves beautifully equipped to deal with a world that no longer exists" – Eric Hoffer.

Change disrupts our comfortable routine and diverts our feeling of security to a fear of the unknown. This fear tells us our once familiar territory will no longer be the same. Therefore, the key is to manage change so it is an opportunity and not a threat. (Newell, 2018)

Leaders are change-makers

Leaders are, by definition, change-makers. When you are called to lead, you must advance, move forward, and improve the situation. The human brain is uniquely attuned to notice changes in our environment, and when it detects a potential threat, the responses are typically: fight, flight, or freeze. Disasters can make or break a leader, yet those who survive typically thrive and flourish (Skipper, 2018). It's important to know that change is something you are subtly learning about all the time as an inevitable part of life, but it's also key to organizational survival.

The pandemic forced education leaders to rise to the challenge and step out of their comfort zones while keeping their communities, employees, and students informed, pausing, restarting daily life, and managing the secondary effects of social and economic disruption. The key to their success was clear, effective, trustworthy communication. Being transparent, honest, and empathetic strengthened relationships and built trust. By anticipating the questions to be asked and consulting experts who could provide factual and supportive information, these leaders were able to dispel rumors, calm emotions, and rally the required resources to navigate the maze of uncertainties. Leaders not only lead others but must manage themselves by staying grounded and clear in a situation that's totally disorienting; otherwise, they will perish. Although this pandemic differs from other crises in our lifetime, learning from it informs the future and helps leaders rebuild to reinvent education.

Leading in times of crisis

The pandemic took a substantial toll on education. It highlighted the vital role our school systems play in daily life, while overnight, both work and school changed. In most cases, "Emergency Remote Learning" ERL (not to be mistaken for true distance learning) was launched without training, understanding, or prior planning causing fear and uncertainty. Based on a report from UNESCO (2020), more than 1.9 billion students worldwide were forced to transfer their education from in-person to online overnight to fight the outbreak of the COVID-19 virus. Emergency Remote learning (ERL) is the unplanned and sudden shift from the traditional form of education into a remote one following a state of emergency (Khlaif et al., 2021). A nation at risk in 1983 did not see this coming, yet we are again faced with designing the future of Pre K-12 education.

The pandemic exposed gaps and disparities in our school systems and accelerated a need to rethink how leaders design schools and instruction and who is at the center of that design: the whole child. Now more than ever, the entire education community must learn from its mistakes to build meaningful, resilient, flexible, engaging learning environments. It's time to break the status quo and lead change rather than be forced into change focused on the whole child's development. Let every voice be heard, most importantly, teachers and students who often are muffled amidst the chaos.

One Small Step

Throughout the pandemic, studies indicated that students fell behind academically because schools needed to prepare to deliver instruction at a distance. Despite a world that thrives on networked telecommunications, most school systems could not pivot seamlessly from an industrial model of "schooling" to a 21st-century model utilizing distance learning theory and methodology. This lack of readiness forced changes that will forever change the fabric of "schooling".

While distance learning is not a new concept, it threatens the comfortable traditional in-person, face-to-face classroom delivery model. Research shows that distance learning has been on the rise for the last two decades (Barbour, 2021), yet most districts consciously ignored the winds of change and were not prepared for virtual learning during the pandemic. This lack of preparation only incited greater concern for the state of the K-12 school system.

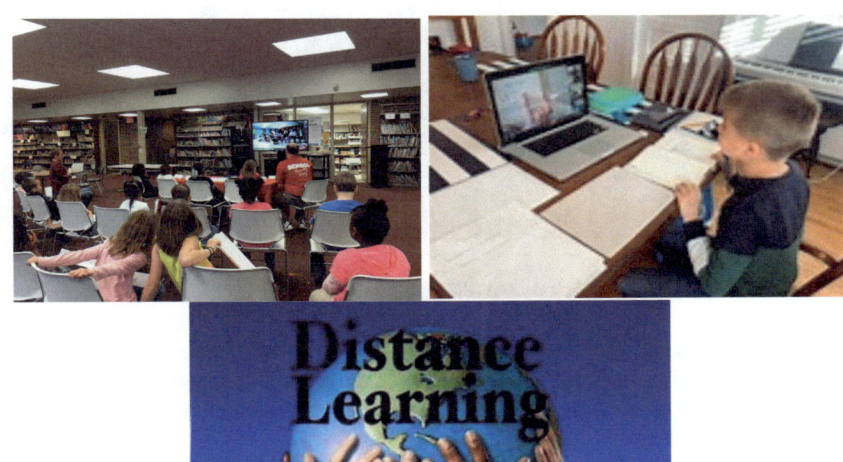

Despite these challenges, district leaders can lead this next level of transformation in education through a shared vision for the future. Regardless of your perspective, the opportunity to embrace these changes is key to equipping students and parents to live, learn, and succeed in the 21st century. The landscape of "school" has changed despite the feelings of isolation, insecurity, anxiety, depression, and fear on the part of students, parents, educators, and the world at large. Most people don't like change; it's just plain hard. However, embracing it and taking action allows school leaders to flourish in these struggling times.

Redesign to Reinvent Education

Closing the achievement gap remains the number one priority of K-12 schools in America. This pandemic crisis, however, can be the opportunity to redesign school systems and instruction that can be individually responsive to the needs of students, thereby ending the "one size fits all" factory model of education. Twenty-first-century learning requires technology and the internet, which cannot be left to chance. Arguably, this is something that schools should have been preparing for and transitioning to these last two decades; however, perceived and real challenges prevailed that stalled progress. Communities and school districts must now level the playing field and focus on supporting the creation of engaging, robust learning opportunities, both in and out of school hours, by utilizing technology-based distance learning methodologies while embracing this change as an opportunity to close the digital divide made fiercely evident by the pandemic. "Staying with the classroom-based school paradigm could permanently destroy our chances of rebuilding our economy and restoring our shrinking middle class to its glory days. Classroom-based education lags far behind when measured against its ability to the creative and agile workforce that the 21st century demands" (Nair, 2018).

My Story - The Big Picture

While never having experienced a pandemic of this magnitude before, I have had the privilege of working with visionary leaders who against all odds, coalesced around common needs in spite of their district differences and demanded a change in the status quo to deliver quality instruction to students across multiple districts. The urgency that brought about this action was not a pandemic but a realization that it was their responsibility to create learning opportunities that would offer their students the opportunity to compete as world-class citizens. These pioneering leaders changed the landscape of K-12 education in the early days of distance learning adoption in Michigan through a shared vision that all children deserve a quality education despite their circumstances.

Despite threats from teacher unions, political hurdles, community pushback, and naysayers' fear of change to the status quo, they set clear expectations, devised a plan, communicated those expectations to all stakeholders, supported the risk-takers, and developed new relationships to ultimately build education telecommunication systems and programming utilizing distance learning technologies serving students K-12. Their pioneering spirit forged the path to creating incredible opportunities for their students, communities, and ultimately the entire state of Michigan that laid the foundation for readiness in the face of the most recent transition overnight to remote learning. Their collective vision of "building a telecommunication pathway to the world" was the impetus behind the creation of SITES (Shiawassee Interactive Telecommunications Education System) and GenNET (Genesee Network for Education Telecommunications)(https://www.gennet.us). Both systems led to the ultimate design and launch of the SEN (Statewide Education Network) (https://www.misen.org) that interconnects all school districts through their regional education service agency in Michigan. Both SITES and GenNET were recognized for innovation by USDLA (United States Distance Learning Association) and the National School Board Association (NSBA) (https://www.youtube.com/watch?v=xX4c9TAxtFA).

Leadership in Action

Opportunity presents itself when you least expect it. And so begins my journey in distance learning in Michigan. Quite by accident, I was recruited to a rural regional education service agency (ISD) in mid-Michigan and SITES in the late 1980s. SITES was the first home-owned/home-grown K-12 fiber-optic telecommunications system in Michigan. Owned and operated by a consortium of nine districts and the ISD, this system paved the way for others in Michigan, modeling collaborative leadership, a shared vision, and the willingness to make changes in the face of adversity while opening doors for students that would otherwise not be opened. Charged with the operations, development, and expansion of distance learning as Director of Technology, my role was to research, design, support, train, and present all aspects of distance learning. This leap of faith helped me grow not only as an educator but a leader in a field dominated by men—technology.

SITES modeled collaboration with stakeholders and blazed the trail for state policy on distance education. It was recognized locally, statewide, and nationally for its innovative approach to meeting the needs of all students, and it laid the foundation for others to follow in Michigan. When I left, SITES was thriving after seven years. Change sees three types of people – people who make things happen, people who watch things happen, and finally those who look around and wonder what happened! I moved on to make other things happen in Genesee County.

Making a Difference

My next chapter brought me to GenNET and the opportunity to design and implement a 450-mile high-speed fiber optic telecommunications system interconnecting 22 local districts serving 87,000 students in a neighboring county. The mission was excellence through equity. Through the collective wisdom, courage, and vision of 23 superintendents, the barriers to quality education were broken when students from urban, rural, and suburban districts became scholars and classmates utilizing the first two-way interactive video and ultimately online learning through the GenNET Online Portal. As the Director of Technology and Assistant Superintendent/ Executive Director for GenNET for over sixteen years, it was my distinct privilege to lead the visioning, development, implementation, expansion, curriculum design, and overall operation of the GenNET system. It changed the trajectory of education in this mid-Michigan county and the entire state of Michigan forever, paving the way toward a more seamless transition to online/virtual learning during the pandemic

Outstanding Leadership Award received 2023 by Education 2.0

"Change the changeable, accept the unchangeable, and remove yourself from the unacceptable."
— Denis Waitley

Contact Dr. Beverly for a free consultation and exploration of your needs.

Contact Dr. Beverly Knox-Pipes
Contact her at https://www.linkedin.com/in/beverlyknox-pipes/

Dr. Jerri-Lynn Williams-Harper
Leader of Educational Change, Management, and Accountability

Dr. Harper has served as Superintendent of Schools in four school districts, as a curriculum specialist, and as an administrator of Charter and Catholic Schools. Dr. Harper is a change agent. She is the Administrator for "Future Teachers" and adjunct Professor for Great Basin College in the Department of Education in Ely, Nevada. Leadership, management, and accountability during change management are her platforms. She co-authored "Leadership Styles" in 2010 and advocates for Leaders of color in educational administration as the need for more administrators of color is apparent.

Leadership and Change Management for Public School Entities
By Dr. Jerri-Lynn Williams-Harper

District XXX is an African American predominantly poor school district of about two-thousand students tucked away in a thriving small Midwest town with a collegiate atmosphere due to its highly ranked small college. However, we will also speak of district XXX in the past tense because of an organizational change management plan involving another district School Districts XXX and ZZZ, because both communities did enter into an annexation process with each other. Town XXX established in 1831, was a Mill town. The current population for town XXX is 8000, 65 % White, 29% Black, and 3% two or more; however, the township is 98.4% White. Town ZZZ, established in 1830, is known as a center for culture, creativity, and professionals. Population numbers for ZZZ are 6728, 95% White, 1% Black, 1.8% two or more, and 3% Hispanic.

At the time of the change management/annexation plan, I was the School Superintendent of District XXX. As a superintendent new to the district, it was obvious the school district was in a serious monetary deficit. The severe financial distress, along with underperforming test scores, was abysmal. The mission of revolutionizing education is paramount, so we remain at the forefront of this technological, educational, and social-emotional journey for our industry, allowing us to train and personalize this industry so the marginalized and affluent members of society will be tomorrow's leaders in a brave new world.

Innovative, Transformative Organizational Change

The change management plan introduced the innovative, transformative process of change management involving annexation processes that require a level of systemic implementation. Such a procedure allows for understanding the present organizational structures and how change dynamics can catapult distressed school districts in a positive direction. The organization's focus is to change mindsets and persuade members to embrace characteristics, traits, attitudes, and behaviors deemed beneficial to the organization (Della, 2018). Closing or consolidating schools is a policy often pursued to increase efficiency in education by limiting financial losses, which improves educational quality for students grouped in remaining school buildings (Yoon, Lunienski & Lee, 2018). Annexation processes require skills involving transformation and change management as well as understanding equitable systemic change for fiscally and underperforming challenged school districts.

The change management plan allowed for a smooth transition concerning the annexation process, a form of school district reorganization affecting public school entities' dissolution process. Annexation is when one district attaches another district to itself. The school district to be attached loses its legal entity and becomes a part of the annexing district. The annexation process enables students to still learn in familiar school settings, but now the annexed school district is physically operated and owned by the annexing school district. Successful annexations use change management, which includes procedures, materials, and organizational actions necessary to bring about change in the process whereby an organization meets its objectives. A change management plan is involved and precise. Change management plans "involve problem-solving in a concerted effort to adapt to changing management needs" (Van Tiem, Mosely, & Dessinger, 2012, p. 624).

Change management is, by default, also a process that intuitively involves learning with due allowance for some failure as business becomes more complex, challenging, and globally competitive; excelling in this dynamic environment requires more understanding, knowledge pragmatism, and collaboration for lasting impact astute change leaders examine and drive their own and other's best practices (Sohmen, p.104, 2016). Using a change management model to improve the annexation process suggests that these changes and suggestions are a compilation of best practices to continue providing public school entities in distress and maintaining an educational presence in their respective communities.

In preparation for change management, the research plans to guide questions and plans are necessary for both the annexing district and the district to be annexed. Bridges (2009) developed the transitional Model of change theory, which focuses on three states of transition that people and organizations go through as they navigate change: (a) Ending, Losing, and Letting Go; (b) The Neutral Zone; and The New Beginning (McDonald, 2018, p.15). Bridges' theory follows Lewin's theory in that we must freeze how the business continues, find a new way of business theory and ethics, and then refreeze the latest methodology and pedagogy once new approaches and plans are acceptable.

Improvements in the Annexation Process through change management include theoretical frameworks based upon three types of change: ADKAR, Kotter, Lewin, and general systems theory models, as they support change through frameworks beneficial to transformational leadership using a change management system. Change management plans depict transitions of roles, leadership, and new frameworks for new or existing organizations. Annexation is a journey of change and requires clear-cut goals, actions, and pronouncements to its framework of change for maximum effectiveness.

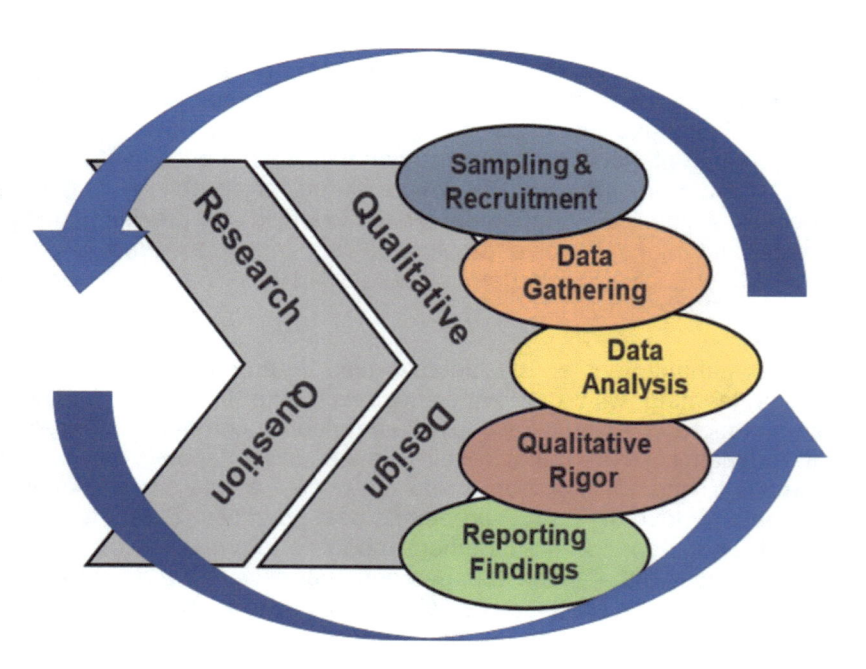

All the systems will be two-dimensional, based on the business and the personal side of change. ADKAR stands for **Awareness** of the business reasons for a change, **Desire** to engage in and participate in change, **Knowledge** about how to change, **Ability** to realize or implement the difference, and **Reinforcement** to ensure change efforts remain once in place. Successful change results from both dimensions of change maturing simultaneously (PROSCI ADKAR MODEL n.d.). The system view looks at the world in terms of relationship and integration. The minor units of the change are integrated based on the flexible and stable manifestations of underlying processes (Mitchell, 2015).

Lewin's Model suggests change is flexible and fluid in three states: change, freeze, and unfreeze. General Systems Theory author Ludwig von Bertalanffy reminds us that constructs and systems are structures influenced by their environments and, therefore, are cognitive structures that communicate valuable characteristics. Kotter's Model provides a roadmap that begins with defining the urgency for change to start by forming a powerful contingent strategy that changes specific communication of new behaviors, removing obstacles, short-term wins, and promoting and challenging transition, and new behaviors become the norm (Calegari, Sibley & Turner, 2015).

ADKAR, Kotter, and Lewin's approaches change similarly and simultaneously on a business and personal level. When two organizations join, each respects the other for the desired outcome during systemic change. Both systems must ebb and flow at the business and the personal level and then mesh at some point. What seems to be important is not what the change is but how the change occurs (Smith, 2016). Kotter espouses creating the climate, engaging, and enabling to implement and sustain the new norms (Teixeira, Gregory & Austin, 2017). Engaging and encouraging allow for buy-in as new boundaries are forming. When one part of the system experiences changes, it can positively or negatively affect the entire process. Lewin seems to bring up the rear by suggesting when new norms are in place, they freeze functions or content in real-time. These constructs all advocate that change is a practice. It is crucial to utilize frameworks such as ADKAR, Kotter, Lewin, and general systems theory because they consider the importance of people in effectuating change. All these models foster change dynamics. ADKAR, Kotter, and Lewin's models for change are similar in the Reinforcement of new changes. Change management via change theory depicts a journey; just as annexation is a journey of transformation, it requires clear-cut goals, actions, and pronouncements to all involved so that the difference will be helpful. Systems theory, implemented contextually, effectuates a new normal for an organization.

Presumed Loss and Detachment of Community Identities

As we worked through the annexation process, both boards of education, administrators from both districts and state personnel from the State Department of Education worked as a team to enable the process to proceed without error and address all legalities pertinent to both school communities. However, we soon discovered this would become a community project with several diverse groups from each district. Students became distrustful of the motives of the community and sincerity concerning their education. One school district was white and affluent, with above-average state statistics on tests, and the other was socio-economically challenged and low-performing on educational measures. So, the initial administrative types performing the work understood it was paramount to enlarge the group of stakeholders because racial issues were becoming apparent, and each community became hostile and protective of its rules and procedures.

This attempt to solve this issue failed because people were being blindsided by issues of racism. All were unprepared for this to become an issue for parents and both communities. These racial issues proved difficult for students because they were open-minded. These students needed to be included in the decision-making and emerged as peacemakers. The target audience will consist of the following: community groups providing input, individuals seeking to contribute information or understand the process and impact of annexation, seekers of how new actions are impactful to the school community, community-at-large, students, parents, and businesses of both communities. Annexation plans were available for both communities in public forums.

Intimidation, Fear, and Resentment of Change

The initial transformation occurred when the high school dissolved and merged with the other secondary school districts 9-12. Once the high schools joined, the community initiating the annexation changed into a K-8 district. Over five years, both communities began assimilating, sharing buildings, materials, and equipment in both towns—the more affluent neighborhood essentially bought out the lower socio-economic school district. Facilities were involved in physical transformations in both cities, and teachers could choose which community was most conducive to their teaching styles and methodologies.

Dealing with the unpredicted race issues and perceptions was sometimes exhausting and scary. One superintendent was African-American, and the other was White. The African-American Superintendent being perceived as an "Uncle Tom" for selling out the minority district to a white community was disconcerting, and physical harm and threats were abundant. The minority superintendent eventually resigned after four years because of the continued hostility and fear of being unsafe. Before the actual resignation, both superintendents ensured that there was a roadmap for the success of both communities of students. At the time of this writing, the annexation continued to strive, and five years into the annexation, the affluent district had its first African-American Valedictorian from the annexed town.

Educational Equity and Accountability

For there to be total success and acceptance for these two school entities, adults must change their prejudicial thoughts and behaviors if the students of these two communities are to thrive and make a positive impact as they move through life. How do we address efficiency, educational quality, and student well-being without racism?

Contact Dr. Jerri Williams
Contact Me: jwilliams434@capellauniversity.edu

ED. Matadores

GIVING A VOICE

María Angélica Benavides, EdD (Dr. B.)

Ambassador Dr. Maria Angelica Benavides (Dr. B.), the Ultimate Legacy Builder, is a renowned global publisher, visionary female leader, accomplished networker, international speaker, and dedicated educator. My certifications are Associate in Arts, Bachelor of Interdisciplinary, Master of Science, and Doctoral Leadership with a Specialization in Curriculum & Instruction. These don't define me but shape who I am now. She has always been curious about Learning Theories, Human Development, and how the brain functions. Dr. B. dedicated a decade to researching and discovering how humans learn and develop and how we can shift our beliefs to shift our decision-making and actions. She catalyzes change; Dr. B embodies resilience, dynamism, and empowerment.

She is passionate about serving all students, including students with special needs, through an online academy and entrepreneurship career path. Her significant goal is to live and leave a legacy for future generations. THROUGH EDUCATION AND CONNECTIONS, Dr. B. supercharges women business owners' mindsets and finances. She adds a beautiful component of spiritual service, helping all individuals align with their higher self through metaphysical practices and tools.

Beyond Labels:
Nurturing Creative Voices, Inspiring Youthpreneurship, and Transforming Education
By María Angélica Benavides, Ed.D.

In the ever-evolving landscape of education, the significance of writing skills cannot be overstated. However, a pressing concern looms over our educational system — a noticeable gap in developing proficient writers among our youth. Despite writing being a cornerstone of education, many students struggle to master this essential skill.

The question that begs attention is: How can we revolutionize the educational system to nurture not just competent but exceptional writers?

A Paradigm Shift is Needed to Cultivate Writing Proficiency

As we delve into the intricacies of this issue, it becomes apparent that the conventional methods of teaching writing need to be revised. Students, burdened with uninspiring assignments, often need help to grasp the true essence of creative expression and effective communication. The consequences are far-reaching, affecting academic performance and hindering personal and professional growth. It's evident a paradigm shift is needed to address the shortcomings in cultivating writing proficiency among our young learners.

Paving the Way for the Generation of Skilled Wordsmiths

To bridge this gap and pave the way for a generation of skilled wordsmiths, our focus must shift toward innovative and engaging approaches. One transformative solution lies in empowering students to become published authors at a young age. By encouraging children and collaborating with teachers to compile their writings into a collective book, we not only celebrate their achievements but also instill a sense of pride and confidence in their writing abilities. This approach goes beyond traditional assessments, fostering an environment where creativity flourishes. We are not just teaching writing skills but creating young entrepreneurs and a love for reading and writing.

Furthermore, inspiring these budding writers to embrace the world of publishing can serve as a catalyst for lifelong learning. Introducing the concept of young authors can ignite a passion for writing and storytelling, propelling students to explore and share their unique voices. In this chapter, we will explore the methods and strategies to revolutionize the teaching of writing, encouraging both educators and students to embark on a journey that transcends the boundaries of conventional education.

Struggling in School and Disliking Writing Led Me to Who I Am Today

In my three decades as an educator, a recurring observation has been the tendency to label students with terms like "at-risk" or "learning disabilities." Rather than embracing these labels, our focus should shift towards cultivating a culture of inspiration, particularly in the realms of reading and writing. Fostering a love for reading is the gateway to becoming a proficient writer.

By immersing students in a world of literature, we enhance their reading skills and lay the foundation for solid writing abilities. Reading is the cornerstone, providing them with a diverse vocabulary, varied writing styles, and imaginative perspectives. However, the challenge lies in encouraging them to read and inspiring them to write and share their unique voices.

Diving Into the Transformative Power of Fostering a Love for Reading, Writing, and Authorship

One effective strategy is to create a supportive community through reading clubs. These clubs can serve as platforms where students explore the joy of reading together and share their published pieces. Engaging in discussions and providing feedback within this community nurture a love for writing and builds confidence in expressing oneself.

This chapter will delve into the transformative power of fostering a love for reading as a catalyst for writing proficiency. By integrating reading clubs and encouraging the sharing of published material, we aim to break free from limiting labels and instead inspire a generation of enthusiastic and skilled readers and writers.

A Quest For Solutions

As a bilingual student who once grappled with a deep-seated disdain for school, I often found myself questioning my own abilities, wondering if a learning disability was the culprit. This personal journey led me to explore Behavioral Theory, Constructivism Theory, Cognitivism Theory, and Learning Theories, seeking answers to the pervasive question of why some students, including myself, struggled to engage with education.

In this quest, a profound realization unfolded—that every child possesses an innate learning capacity. Breaking free from the constraints of perceived disabilities, I transitioned from a place of self-doubt to a love for learning. This transformative experience fueled my commitment to education, leading me to specialize as a special education director for over 19 years a total of 30+ years in education.

Stop Pigeonholing Students and Embrace Innovation

We should embark on a journey that transcends labels and embraces innovation. Rather than pigeonholing students with learning disabilities, we focus on discovering alternative methods to kindle their love for learning, especially in reading and writing. The revelation that everyone harbors the potential to learn became the cornerstone of my approach, and it echoes through the template I've developed—a strategy designed to unlock the writing skills within both children and adults.

During the challenging times of the COVID-19 pandemic, I witnessed a collective desire among many to express themselves through writing. Yet, the obstacle remained in knowing what to write and how to do so effectively. Within this context, the template created becomes a beacon of guidance for those interested in writing and publishing. This template is more than a tool; it's an invitation to tap into the rich reservoir of creativity within, enabling individuals to not only become writers but to publish their unique works of art proudly. In essence, it's a roadmap for anyone, regardless of age or background, to share their voices with the world, transforming personal stories into powerful narratives that resonate beyond the confines of the individual experience.

Catalyst Strategies
Below are three strategies for teaching children to become better writers and, at the same time, help teachers publish their writing pieces.

Interactive Writing Workshops:
Foster a dynamic learning environment by organizing interactive writing workshops for children. Encourage creativity and expression through engaging prompts and activities. Provide constructive feedback to guide them in refining their writing skills. Simultaneously, extend these workshops to teachers, creating a collaborative space where educators can share their own writing pieces. This two-way interaction enhances students' writing abilities and empowers teachers to contribute to the culture of creativity and publication.

Literary Clubs and Peer Review Sessions:
Establish literary clubs within the school where students can come together to discuss, share, and celebrate their written works. Encourage peer review sessions, where students provide feedback on each other's writing. This not only strengthens their writing skills through diverse perspectives but also cultivates a sense of community. Extend this concept to teachers, fostering a supportive network for educators to share and refine their writing pieces. The exchange of ideas and constructive critiques within these clubs becomes a catalyst for improvement.

Integrated Publishing Projects:
Implement integrated publishing projects that involve both students and teachers in the process of creating a collective publication. This could be a school magazine, anthology, or digital platform showcasing the creative works of the school community. Guide students in writing, editing, and presenting their pieces. Simultaneously, offers teachers the opportunity to contribute and collaborate on the publication. This joint effort instills a sense of accomplishment in students and empowers teachers to showcase their writing skills. The tangible outcome of a shared publication reinforces the idea that everyone, regardless of age or role, has a valuable voice to share with the broader community.

G0 Beyond Teaching, Learning, and Publishing

Integrating fundraising initiatives with student publications is a brilliant way to not only inspire passion for writing but also instill a sense of entrepreneurship. By allowing students to sell their books through fundraising efforts, you create a platform for what could be termed "Youthpreneurship." This innovative approach fosters financial literacy and empowers students to take pride in their creative work.

The dual benefit of students making money from their publications while simultaneously raising funds for the school creates a symbiotic relationship. It teaches valuable skills such as marketing, communication, and teamwork as students collaborate on fundraising projects. Moreover, the tangible outcome of selling their published works reinforces the idea that their voices and creations have real-world value.

Transformative Journey From the Traditional Paradigms of Education

In conclusion, this chapter embarks on a transformative journey from the traditional education paradigms, shedding labels and embracing innovation. Recognizing the innate capacity of every child to learn, we have explored strategies to nurture a love for reading and writing, transcending the limitations of perceived disabilities. The journey has been personal, shaped by experiences as a struggling and bilingual student, an educator, and a director in special education.

The chapter unfolds an opportunity to connect with me to gain knowledge in my template designed to unlock the writing skills within children and adults alike, providing a roadmap for self-expression and creativity. Beyond the confines of individual experiences, it encourages sharing voices with the world, fostering a culture of publication that extends to both students and teachers.

Furthermore, integrating fundraising initiatives adds a dynamic layer to the narrative, introducing the concept of "Youthpreneurship." Students become better writers and entrepreneurs, earning money through creative endeavors and contributing to the school's financial growth.

Let's advocate for a holistic approach to education that transcends conventional boundaries, inspires a passion for learning, and empowers students to become confident readers, writers, and entrepreneurs. By embracing innovation, collaboration, and the celebration of diverse voices, we pave the way for a future where education is not just a means of imparting knowledge but a catalyst for personal and collective transformation.

Offer Get It Today

Steps to Build Success from Scratch

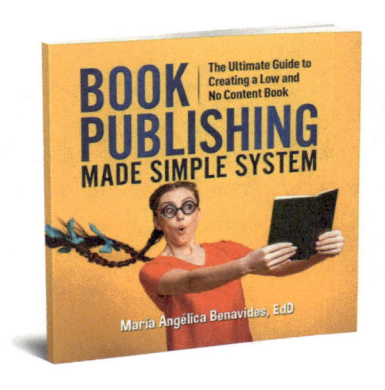

Become the published author you have always wanted to be. The benefits of writing and publishing a book are to leave a legacy, change lives, write to heal old wounds, earn money from profits, speak and get on other people's platforms, and become an authority in your field. Start

with low and no-content books that are not your traditional books. A low and no content book has a limited amount of writing or text in it. Get your copy of the Book Publishing Made Simple System book on Amazon.
- Find a niche and research it to have a better understanding
- Design a sizzling book cover to attract the audience's attention
- Choose a dynamic book title
- Create your low-content or no-content pages
- Get my mini 5X5 book Book Publishing Made Simple System

Free Gift

I help entrepreneurs find that story and tell it to the world by writing a book and creating your signature talk to help you overcome the wounds of the past.

Telling your story can be cathartic and makes you grow as a person, gives you satisfaction, and allows you to increase your chances of success. It takes you out of that dark area that perhaps you thought ruined your life forever. It shows you the light. Share your light with others who are waiting for your life-transforming message. You will leave this experience with a feeling of dominance.

You are here to make a big difference in the world. The best way to do this is to use your story, experience, knowledge, and advice to help others be successful. This strategy that I share with you will guide you in a process so that through your story you can package and share advice, systems, tools and processes, and create a lucrative business that impacts lives. Plus, leave a legacy that outlives you!

ED. Matadores

Get my free **4-Online Video Series** below called Book Publishing Made Simple System so you can start writing your book or start with a low-content book that is a notebook or journal.

I have learned from giants such as Anthony Robbins, Dean Graziosi, John Maxwell, Grant Cardone, Forbes Riley, Bill Walsh, and Mark Victor Hansen to help me think bigger, make more significant decisions, and take giant action steps toward my mission to millions. I now create even more success for business women owners. I specialize in publishing books, business programs, speaker training programs, certification programs, and global masterminds. I put the best resources every business needs to learn about to survive and thrive in any economy. My message has been delivered as cutting-edge content.

ED. Matadores

Dr. Maria Rodriguez
Founder and CEO of Care Counseling Center

Dr. Maria Rodriguez is an accomplished mental health professional dedicated to a compassion-first approach to helping immigrant individuals, children, and families adapt and thrive in the United States. She is recognized as a Top 25 executives of New Jersey and a Global Outstanding Leader in Health Care. Dr. Rodriguez has an extensive academic background which has been fortified with numerous accolades. With a Master's Degree in Clinical Psychology from William Paterson University and a Ph.D. in General Psychology from Capella University, she further solidified her expertise with 18 years of experience as an Adjunct Professor of Women's and Gender Studies and Psychology. Across her notable career, she has amassed over two decades of hands-on experience in mental health counseling, providing invaluable support to diverse populations.

As a first-generation American with Dominican parents, she has cultivated a deep understanding of the myriad of challenges immigrants face as they work toward realizing their ambitious goals in a new home. Her innate sense of hope for her community led her to establish the Care Counseling Center (awarded the Best of Somerville New Jersey in 2022 and 2023) – a safe space providing support for emotional trauma, legal complexities, and practical issues that immigrants may face in addition to helping families and individuals from various backgrounds.

Give Everyone A Voice
By Dr. Maria Rodriguez

Our educational system stands at a crossroads in a world that thrives on innovation, interconnectedness, and rapid change. As we all know, schools struggle with underfunding, unengaged teachers, unengaged parents, unengaged administrations, and most importantly, bored, stressed, disconnected students from the most affluent of neighborhoods to the most challenging of "Title" schools placed in the middle of already challenged neighborhoods.

We find ourselves in a time of both challenge and opportunity. The cracks in the foundation of our traditional education system have deepened, leaving room for doubt and skepticism to creep in. We see it at school board meetings and on social media pages run by students, filled with longing comments for the community. We see where things have gotten us.

I am Dr. Maria Rodriguez, a passionate advocate for educational reform and the founder of the CARE Counseling Center. My life's work has been a testament to the belief that every student, regardless of background or circumstance, has the right to an education that empowers and uplifts. I act as an interested party for students and parents who wouldn't have a voice or be able to make informed choices.

I stand firm in my commitment to guiding this revolution from a position of empathy and expertise in working with mental health.

The Care Counseling Center

The CARE Counseling Center, my organization, extends its nurturing embrace to children, especially immigrants, who might grapple with language barriers and cultural nuances that often hinder their educational voyage to the United States. With an unwavering dedication to fostering holistic growth, the center addresses linguistic barriers and seeks to bridge the gap between cultures, allowing these young minds to flourish in a welcoming and inclusive environment. Our mission is not only to teach but to empower, to not merely instruct but to inspire, ensuring that every child, regardless of his or her background, can embark on the education path with confidence and hope.

ED. Matadores

Care Counseling Center and the Ed Matadores

The Ed Matadores' mission of revolutionizing the educational system resonates deeply with the core principles that drive the CARE Counseling Center's endeavors. Our educational system is a pivotal foundation for shaping future generations, and its current shortcomings perpetuate disparities that hinder progress and social mobility. The urgency to transform this system lies not only in its academic inadequacies but also in its impact on our young learners' emotional and psychological well-being.

By reimagining education as a holistic journey that fosters intellectual curiosity, emotional resilience, and cultural understanding, we pave the way for a not only knowledgeable but compassionate, adaptable, and inclusive society. The Ed Matadores' commitment mirrors our own, acknowledging that the transformation of education transcends textbooks and classrooms, embracing the unique needs of each student and championing an ecosystem where educators are empowered to ignite the spark of curiosity and lifelong learning.

In essence, the mission is vital because it is a call to cultivate an educational landscape that molds not just capable professionals but empathetic citizens and trailblazers who will shape the future with vision, compassion, and innovation in integrated, safe, welcoming communities that never tolerate hate, inequity, or lack of diversity.

No More "Disadvantaged" Status

In our journey to transform education, we must confront students' challenges, particularly those from disadvantaged backgrounds. These challenges include inadequate funding for schools in low-income areas, which leads to outdated materials, limited resources, and fewer extracurricular activities. This impacts the overall quality of education and restricts students' growth opportunities. Additionally, limited access to qualified teachers results in larger classes and a lack of personalized instruction, hindering students' learning experiences.

It all starts with the labels put on these schools.
- "Inner-city"
- "Title One"
- "Challenged"

Imagine being called those names. You would not have the drive to succeed if your child's school was already branded as a hard or lost cause.

Time to Make Schools More Welcoming

Outdated facilities create uncomfortable learning environments that affect motivation. At the same time, insufficient resources such as technology and textbooks hinder students' ability to keep up with modern educational standards. Getting past these obstacles, students facing poverty often deal with challenging home situations like unstable housing and food insecurity, which impact their readiness to learn. In essence, making schools more welcoming goes beyond cosmetic changes to the physical environment; it involves a comprehensive approach that tackles issues ranging from infrastructure to resource accessibility and addresses the diverse challenges students face outside the classroom. By creating a supportive and nurturing educational ecosystem, we not only enhance the learning experience for individual students but also contribute to building a foundation for a more equitable and prosperous society. It's an investment in the future, recognizing that the potential for success lies in the empowerment and well-being of each and every student.

When home and school aren't welcoming, where can a child feel safe to learn and grow?

The Biggest Obstacle: Language

Language barriers pose another obstacle, especially for students from diverse linguistic backgrounds, as schools may lack resources for English as a Second Language (ESL) programs. Immigrant families encounter unique barriers this way. For example, put yourself in their shoes. You've moved to a new place and can barely understand or speak the language – you still have to care for, feed, clothe, and keep a roof over your family. It is easy to imagine that showing up at school events or making sure your child's homework is done would fall behind quickly.

Limited English understanding and cultural differences can hinder teacher communication and integration into the school community. These families may struggle to access information about available resources and navigate the complex education system of their new country.

CARE Counseling Center in the Community

Recognizing that families and children are often unfairly boxed into predefined categories, I embarked on a journey to provide targeted interventions that catered to their unique needs. Our personalized support system sought to dissolve labels, replacing them with comprehensive strategies to address social, emotional, and academic challenges. This initiative was rooted in rigorous research demonstrating the profound impact of personalized support on students' well-being and success. Through counseling, mentorship, and targeted resources, we aimed to rewrite the narrative, transforming families' experiences within the education system.

Intensive In-Community Service (IIC), our service, is an incisive, goal-oriented, and needs-based clinical intervention that addresses the emotional and behavioral challenges of youth with moderate to high needs. It may be provided in a youth's home or an amenable community location by a licensed behavioral health clinician and is intended to stabilize and support the youth and family to deter more intensive interventions and to support the youth and family in collaboration with the Child Family Team (CFT) or identified support system.

Intensive In-Community Service (IIC) is a short-term, solution-focused intervention that addresses presenting behaviors resulting in the youth and her/his family/caregiver/guardian gaining insight and improving function at home and in the community. Youth and families can receive Intensive In-Community Services if they receive Care Management, MRSS services, or Treatment Home Stabilization Services through the New Jersey Children's System of Care.

In the maze of educational reform, I have discovered that the most profound transformations often come from our relentless commitment to stand alongside families and children facing challenges within our flawed system. As the owner and operator of the CARE Counseling Center, I have found myself attending school meetings as a beacon of support and a bridge of translation, bearing witness to the unspoken struggles that unfold behind the scenes. What I have observed time and again is a profoundly ingrained label that sticks like glue. Once a family or child is branded with a problem, that label seems to linger, regardless of progress or potential. But within the cracks of this flawed framework, I have discovered the potential for innovative initiatives built upon a foundation of empathy, inclusivity, and personalized support.

Your Story, My Story, Their Journey: A Journey of Transformation

The journey of implementing this initiative was both inspiring and challenging. Collaborating with educators, administrators, and parents, we navigated the terrain of resistance and skepticism, presenting a vision of change that embraced every child's individuality – we were acting as a translator and voice in our capacity – it was up to the child and family to make use of us as a tool. Over time, we garnered support and buy-in by emphasizing the potential for improved student outcomes and enhanced teacher-student relationships. Implementing this transformation took dedication and persistence. It was a path of many milestones, from designing personalized learning plans to training educators in trauma-informed approaches and culturally sensitive strategies. This approach required a significant investment of time, resources, and collaboration. Still, the impact on students' lives was immeasurable, starting with one school and changing to many more. The "problem" brand can be lifted if a community sees it isn't true.

Your Call for Revolution: Bridging the Gap

True transformation can't flourish in isolation. We have to be in it together.

For others to readily implement similar initiatives, systemic changes are imperative. We must reevaluate how labels and stigma are perpetuated within the educational system and champion a culture of continuous improvement that celebrates diversity and individuality. Teachers, parents, administrators, and policymakers must come together to recognize that a one-size-fits-all approach fails to serve the varied needs of our students. By investing in professional development, creating safe spaces for collaboration, and promoting mental health resources, we can dismantle barriers and create an ecosystem where personalized support thrives.

To address these challenges, we can implement strategies like cultural sensitivity training for educators, offering multilingual resources, establishing partnerships with community organizations, creating opportunities for parental engagement, and providing mentorship programs. By fostering inclusive environments, offering language access, and ensuring equal access to resources, we can pave the way for a transformative educational experience that supports the growth and success of all students, regardless of their background.

ED. Matadores

When it comes to education, change is inevitable. Still, it is up to us to weave it with intention and empathy and not the way of cold-hearted callousness in the way that I sometimes fear it is going.

The story of my journey with the CARE Counseling Center illustrates the profound impact that arises when we dare to challenge the status quo. As we work together to revolutionize the educational system, let us remember that the power of transformation lies within our collective determination to create an inclusive and nurturing environment that fosters every child's growth and potential.

Today, you can reach Dr. Maria via her websites, MariaRodriguez.org & CareCounselingCenter.org for in-person and virtual wellness services centered on resolving conflicts in self, business, and relationships.

For a free consultation, please contact info@carecounselingcenter.org. Success is often accompanied by challenges and setbacks. Mental health services can equip you with the tools to build resilience, enabling you to bounce back from failures and navigate obstacles more effectively. A resilient mindset is key to overcoming the inevitable hurdles on the path to success. The keys to unlocking your success are waiting.

ED. Matadores

Trish Persen MEd, MFA

Trish Persen is the author of *Shift Your Narrative in 28 Days,* a journey of self-discovery through the power of reflection. Winner of Stage 32 2nd Annual TV Drama Pilot competition with #DeathByShakespeare. She is a published poet in various International Library of Poets anthologies. Trish holds advanced degrees in both Education and Creative Writing. She currently teaches creative hopefuls at Full Sail University and LA Film School.

Recognizing The Power Of Collective Communication: Taming The Stubborn Bull And Unveiling The Big Why In Education
By Trish Persen

As I embarked on my journey through the halls of academia, I quickly realized that education is not just about institutions and degrees; it's about the profound wisdom we can all contribute, regardless of our backgrounds or levels of experience. Allow me to share the transformative power of some important principles that have guided my own path and continue to inspire my work in revolutionizing the educational system.

Taming the Stubborn Bull

Education is my life. I teach at a university in Winter Park, FL, and a film school in Los Angeles, CA. Both institutions consist of creatively diverse hopefuls who wish to follow their dreams of entering the Entertainment Industry. The ages range from just fresh out of high school until retirement age. It is quite an interesting dynamic to have that mix in my classes. We all have the wisdom to carry, and each one of us adds to the value of the course no matter what level of experience. Each classroom has an opportunity to foster a sense of community and mutual encouragement that transcends the traditional boundaries of learning. The encouragement of building relationships and forging a community is inspired in each class. This is the mindset I bring to the table. Communication is the foundation for everything. Communication, I discovered, is the bedrock upon which all educational revolutions are built. We are blessed to be the only species with the power of linguistics. Our words have weight; we need to recognize what that means, especially in the age of technology. We must recognize the words we tell ourselves to carry the most weight.

ED. Matadors are the warriors on the front line, the innovators wishing to change the face of education and break down the barriers that keep us from having the voice to receive what is needed. Taming the stubborn "Bull" of broken systems will not come without scars, but the spirit of the fight will keep many from returning into the pit. That is why I am here, and I am honored to be among so many strong educators willing to face the "Bull" as a collective and win.

Unveiling the Big "WHY" to Empower Student Voices and Education Access

As educators, we need to shatter the formidable barriers that have long denied students their rightful voices and access to the education they deserve. In our quest for transformation, we confront a fierce adversary— the stubborn, unyielding bull that represents the broken systems of education. It starts at the core. It is one thing to make the decision to go back to school, but it is another to be successful at it. Just like any big decision in life, the excitement can wear off unless you understand the "WHY" you are doing it in the first place.

The first point of communication is our "WHY." The problem is that we look for external sources to tell us this when the answer is inside us. If we are making a decision based on the happiness/appeasement of others, we are compromising what is truly meant for us. The conversation needs to happen within us first. We must explore the true reason behind our decision and remember what has brought us here to keep moving forward. We must be conscious of the journey ahead and that we are the leaders of that journey. Validation needs to come from within. The problem is many of us do not know how to communicate with others, let alone ourselves. I witness this in my classes all the time when students are asked to explain WHY something happens when the thoughts in their heads try to manifest and come out of their mouths. The "WHY" somehow gets lost in translation, and this is where the self-doubt starts creeping in. If this continues right out the gate, a spiral of negative, defeated energy will travel with them until they quit. The conversation needs to happen within first. I will say this until the end of time. The power of reflection will forever be my stand on inner growth and a journey of success. I only discovered this after doing it backward for so long in my own journey. I needed to reflect on how the system was set up and how my class was structured. I asked them to know their audience when their first audience member was on the other side of their brains. I started to frame it using the lingo of the entertainment industry and had a conversation about the "Origin Story." Marvel has done it with almost every character, and I had a revelation.

What better way to find their "WHY" than by reflecting on their origin story? I ask them to dive deeply into their childhood and recall something that may have led them to where they currently are. Many started out with perplexity on their faces, and then I would give them an example. "Picture this at seven, eating a bowl of Frosted Flakes" in front of the TV. In awe, you see "Woody" and "Buzz LightYear" for the first time. Maybe you did not notice it then, but this point of reflection tells you at that moment, you felt as if you had friends. In that moment, something tingly was happening in your heart, and you were happy. Upon reflecting, you understand that a passion was invited inside you to one day create characters that would make 7-year-olds just like you feel as if they had friends, too." You can hear the light bulbs go on as I would say, "That, my friends, is your WHY…" Think about it. If you have not convinced yourself, how will you be able to convince others? To convey your message to others, you must understand it for yourself.

Once this is understood, I witness an amazing transformation. The sense of community becomes second nature. The desire to use the platform and their voices are exciting. They begin to see their potential not only with their eyes but also with their hearts. Every step and task becomes a new opportunity to feed his or her WHY. The results in just four weeks' time are that the foundation is laid out for the rest of their journey towards graduation and beyond. This is a template for the rest of the world. Join us as we embark on a journey to tame this relentless beast and unveil the solutions that will revolutionize education for all.

Evoking the power of your inner voice

The journey through introspection came with experience. I was unaware of what I was doing until I was asked to share the knowledge. Some values are designed within us and are innately initiated through our actions. We do them with such ease that our conscious minds do not pay attention to the potential of that power. Sharing knowledge was something that I never had to think about consciously. The desire to be inspired and to inspire others was something that "just was." I did not realize that while giving my knowledge to others, I forgot to give back to myself. This is the core of the problem. Not only are we not hearing each other, we are not hearing the power of our own thoughts. The story that we dismiss for ourselves is the story that we will continue to dismiss for others.

I caught myself using the language that I believed defined who I am. Using this language was placing a limit on my abilities. When asked, "Who are you?" My first answer would be an educator. This was natural, but what I did not realize is that just because it was "natural" did not mean I wasn't capable of anything else. However, it painted a safe little neat box for me. I did not have to prove that I was an educator. I just was. I realize the power I gave to being an educator is the same power I have to be anything else that I desire. I just needed to choose to listen to my inner voice.

My signature line for emails is "Be Inspired." This mainly started as a closing for correspondence with my students and later started to become a staple in how I end an email. Again this was "natural." I did not recognize the impact those simple words would have. Over the years, many students have commented on how those two words change their mindset. It only took me over a decade to figure out what those two words mean to me and my daily direction. Words hold weight; recognize that power and be gentle.

We all carry wisdom

In today's society, we are blinded by thinking we are experts at everything just because we have read a few sentences from an article on Twitter. We think we know when, in reality, we do not know everything. This is the ignorance of the Human Race. Knowledge is a gift. Divine knowledge is infinite. How could one person carry all that knowledge? The short answer is they cannot. That is why we are different. We all carry wisdom, shared through experience and connected by emotion. Emotions are how we recognize each other as another human. This is the breakdown of communication. Unfortunately, we tend to view this gift as only a right and not a privilege. We take for granted that with great power comes even greater responsibility. Communication is a derivative of the Latin word *communicare,* meaning to exchange information. When we believe our story is the only *true* story, then we close off any chance of gaining perspective. We become dismissive of each other's experience and even existence. This behavior is a virus that infects all platforms. It is not only in education, but education is where it needs to change first. We are preconditioned to believe that our experiences are the only experiences. Our beliefs are the only beliefs we have because that is what we were unconsciously told was true. There would be no other way; there could be no one else experiencing this, and yet there is.

My Call for P.E.A.C.E.
Gaining perspective is freedom

In conclusion, as we reflect on the journey through my educational background, the power of wisdom, community, and communication has illuminated the path of progress. The Ed Matdores stand as warriors, ready to confront the bull of a broken system and usher in a new era of educational excellence. Together, we have the strength, the passion, and the solutions to reshape the landscape of education, ensuring that every voice is heard and every student receives the opportunities they rightfully deserve. The revolution has begun; we are the vanguard, committed to a better future for all.

My call to action is for a global shift in how we view each other in the world. Understanding that we are all on this planet collectively for a purpose. We have a responsibility as carriers of knowledge to share it with each other and provide missing pieces of the infinite knowledge we all possess. Our language, demographics, religion, gender, and even our story were not meant to be the same. We needed diversity to understand all layers of life. The universal language is LOVE. We EXIST on this planet together. No one has the power to dismiss any other being's existence, ever! We do not have to live the same, which is what is so beautiful about being a human. Gaining perspective is freedom. Being free to understand that it is okay not to be the same. Our species is bigger than the region we were born into or the skin that covers our souls. This understanding does not happen unless we learn how to communicate with each other. It is infuriating that we are now in an age where we can just reach into our back pockets and pull out a device that will connect us anywhere in the world, and we do not readily use this amazing tool properly. We need to go back to the roots of communication and realize that it is an exchange of information. This is my call for reinvention. This is my call for P.E.A.C.E.

P. E. A. C. E:

P.E.A.C.E

Call for P.E.A.C.E

People evolve allowing communication & educate.

Concept Created by:	Trish Persen
People	Acknowledging the ability to know and understand each other.
Evolve	Open your eyes, ears, and hearts to a new perspective.
Allowing	Giving and receiving permission to share ideas without judgment.
Communication	Discover your voice and learn how to use it wisely.
Educate	Recognize when you have mastered these qualities and pay it forward.

Gaining perspective is freedom

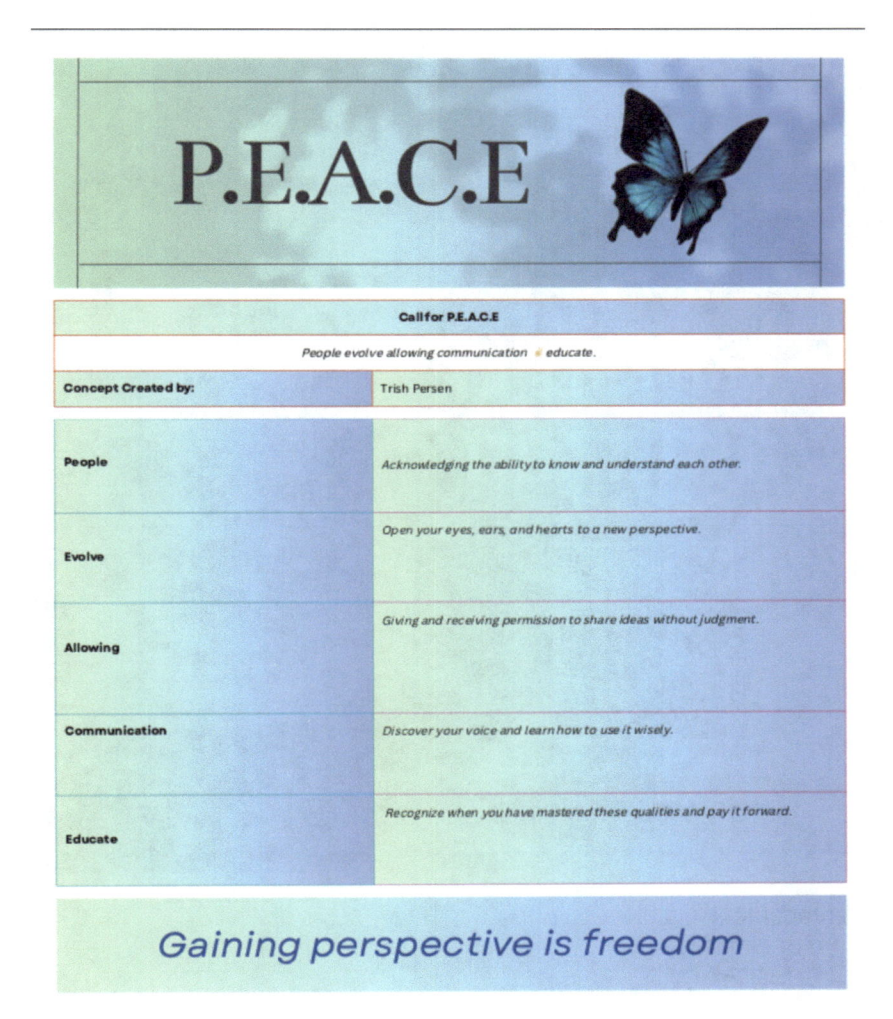

Offer

Before you can learn to speak to others effectively, you must learn to speak effectively to yourself. A journey through introspection is what has given me clarity. Self-reflection empowers you to think differently. Once you are aware of the blocks within, you will gain an awareness of what those could be for others. This will allow you to communicate with a new understanding. I invite you to walk the journey I have embarked on myself. The journal is complemented with a video series that sheds

ED. Matadores

some insight on fear, self-worth, and taking inspired action. Be inspired and step into rediscovering who you really are.

Journal or Online video with QR code

Contact Me
Blinq or Linktree QR

321.848.3610 trishapersen@gmail.com

ED. Matadores

SERVING THE UNDERSERVED

Kai Smith, MBA, MPA (Ph.D/JD Student)

Founding Executive Director of: Gang Diversion, Reentry And Absent Fathers Intervention Clinical Services (501c3) and CEO/Managing Director of: The Collaborative for Better Urban Health, LLC.

Proprietor | CEO | Executive Director | Published Author | Life Coach | Urban Life Skills Expert | Entrepreneur | Public Speaker

Born and raised during the three most nefarious social eras of New York City [the 1970s, 1980s, and 1990s] Kai lived a lifestyle that many of today's accomplished rappers, actors, and screenwriters offer in their blockbuster art. This lifestyle directly resulted in Kai spending 16 consecutive years confined within prisons in 3 different States. Released in 2002, labeled a career criminal. Kai, like other black men, returned to the same decaying community with the same societal ills. He was happy to be home but lost. With six felonies on his criminal record, zero resources, opportunities, very little support, and being written off by society as hopeless, Kai vowed to change not only his life, but the lives of children that would endure what he had just survived. While in prison, Kai designed and created an urban youth services program. He regained his freedom in 2002, and over the past twenty years, coupled with his earning several college degrees, Kai has made a difference in the lives of hundreds of children nationwide. He is the Founding Executive Director of www.GRAAFICS.org and the CEO of www.BetterUrbanHealth.com

There Are No Bad Kids: Effectively Preparing Behaviorally Challenged Urban Youth For Future Success.

Still Facing The Same Problems
By Kai Smith

"*This year, there are going to be millions of children that we needlessly lose. We can save them all. Those of us in education have held on to a business plan that we don't care how many millions of young people fail, we're going to continue to do the same thing that didn't work. No one is saying enough is enough of this business plan that does not work. I grew up in the inner city, and there were kids who were failing 56 years ago when I first went to school. Those same schools are still lousy 56 years later*" (Canada, 2013).

Mr. Canada is the CEO of The Harlem Children's Zone and his TED Talk ten years ago has garnered over 500,000 views. The schools he spoke of then are 66 years old today and are still not making the progress that is needed.

Addressing Violence and Mental Health

I was once a severely behaviorally challenged child in New York City Public Schools, who turned felon. Now as a New York City (NYC) resident, dual business owner, and scholar, I am contracted to deliver services to those same public schools that I once attended. I have dedicated my work to helping poor children of color that attend urban public schools through both of my businesses: The Gang Diversion, Reentry and Absent Fathers Intervention Centers (GRAAFICS) and The Collaborative for Better Urban Health, LLC.

GRAAFICS is a 501c3 established in 2003. It is a four-tiered social-emotional, culturally responsive, trauma-informed prevention and intervention program that offers therapeutically supported behavior redirection and life skill services to youth throughout the nation. In New York, GRAAFICS is the only clinically endorsed, culturally inclusive, education and curriculum-driven behavior modification program that operates within the four tiers: (1) schools, (2) community, (3) detention facilities, and (4) home. As an approved vendor to public schools, we offer multi-dimensional services in forums where students can receive one to two credits toward graduation. The goal of GRAAFICS, as it correlates to the NYC Department of Education, is to reduce violent incidents within schools by using tailored services that teach and empower students to employ social-emotional responsibility, consequential thinking, anger management, and anger replacement. Students in the program are supported by wraparound mental health services. The Collaborative for Better Urban Health, LLC was established in 2020. This company is a multi-service healthcare support agency created to address quality health service voids in communities of color. To provide better services to disenfranchised people, we specialize in pairing our clients with quality healthcare providers reflective of their race, culture, ethnicity, and lived experiences. At Better Urban Health our in-school services consist of one-to-one mental health services for students and staff, clinical professional development for staff, mental health awareness classes, health and wellness classes, and complex trauma screening and services referrals. The goal of Better Urban Health in schools is to address abnormal student and staff behavior that negatively impacts a school's environment.

From Felon to LeaderMaker

For sixty years, the challenge has always been how to effectively educate today's behaviorally challenged students. While incarcerated, I created a behavior management model centered around education and entrepreneurialism designed specifically to serve behaviorally challenged students. This was done by tirelessly studying anger management, anger replacement therapy, and gang diversion models. I juxtaposed those models against one another, applied community trends and data, and then created a model based on both my findings and lived experiences.

Once I exited prison, I enrolled in those colleges that would allow me to build my vision around my lived experiences and what I was currently seeing in communities of color. Nearly twenty-two years and five college degrees later, the Kai Smith model for modifying volatile student behavior and addressing school violence has been used in K-12 schools throughout New York City. The course includes one-to-one and grouped mental health services for students, parents, and staff. My model addresses the challenges of unprovoked impulsive in-school volatile behavior via consequential thinking. It reduces violent incidents both inside and outside school, increases attendance, increases grades, decreases law enforcement & criminal legal system contact, and increases family quality of life. However, we refuse to accept 'band-aid' solutions. While we have demonstrated great success at the micro level, garnering the support to scale the model remains a challenge.

Understanding Students Individually & Collectively

With the subtle eradication of public school courses that taught home economics, etiquette, or habilitation skills, we have several generations of students born from parents who were children themselves, born from uneducated parents, raised in households where there was no appreciation for education, born from parents who are or were criminals themselves, raised in families where 'the man' or 'the system' was at fault for everything, or raised in communities where social determinants of health are so deplorable that they contribute to undiagnosed and normalized complex traumas. These conditions produce behaviors that are perceived as untreatable to the untrained eye. I understand the lifestyle and the behavior because they describe my personal lived experiences. Coupled with this, my life in the streets as a former criminal made me fearless. So, by the time I was finally given an opportunity to present my model to a class filled with students—kids that everyone else was afraid of—I was at home because I was one of those kids. I came from where they came from. I saw what they saw. I felt what they felt and I had done what they were doing.

Today, I am a motivational speaker and professional development trainer, but for years I worked as a consultant for multiple NYC government agencies. Additionally, while pursuing my education, my business model was the centerpiece of each of my four degrees. So, just as globally respected entertainers practice their craft until it is perfected, both my model and its delivery were thoroughly rehearsed long before I introduced them to schools. The model works. In the movie *'Pursuit of Happyness,'* actor Will Smith's character Chris Gardner tells his son, "You got a dream? You go get it. People want to tell you that you can't do something because they can't do it" (2006). When I saw this clip, it spoke directly to me. This is something that my grandma instilled in me almost from birth. As far as what worked? Me! I worked. I was relentless. I challenged mayors and school chancellors. I dared school principals to give me an hour with those students that no one else wanted to deal with. If, by the end of that hour, they didn't see magic before their eyes, I didn't want a contract. But, if they did, not only did I get a contract, but I'd have complete control. It worked every time.

A Model for Success

The initiative was to create a model resembling a dart board, with entrepreneurialism or money, power, and success as the inner bullseye. Why is entrepreneurialism over education? Because 100% of behaviorally challenged students, other than those with an undiagnosed or untreated chronic condition, have goals that directly correlate to money. Money is the universal language. All roads lead to money. The rest of the board depicts the student's educational journey: the double ring around the outside edge represents day one of class, the triple ring represents successfully completing high school, and the outer bullseye represents college or another form of higher supplemental education. Under the auspices of life skills and habilitation, we generate supplemental rings which we position throughout the board as stepping-stones. To get student buy-in, we connect the supplemental rings to the positive and negative experiences of the celebrities, rappers, and athletes they follow, juxtaposing the experiences of their idols against their own lives and creating teachable lessons that empower them to think about and practice stronger decision-making.

The Challenge of Changing a System

My biggest challenge has always been financial sponsorship and convincing school principals, district superintendents, and other educational leaders that my services work. Schools have seen all other approaches they have tried to address the violence and most challenging behaviors fall short which makes it difficult for them to believe in the promise of my model despite having supporting success statistics that other programs do not have. Fortunately, I have four superpowers: humility, transparency, vulnerability, and tenacity. I spent years thoroughly investigating the circumstances around the lived experiences of their students' favorite celebrities. I strategically used excerpts from those celebrities' lives where they best fit to convey particular messages. I overcame implementation obstacles by consistently reminding myself of where I came from and how fortunate I am today and tapping into prison memories used as strength reserves to push through tough situations.

Success By the Numbers

Through both GRAAFICS and Better Urban Health, we have been able to work within twenty NYC public schools, directly serving over 600 students. Our outcomes have included:

- 70% decrease in long-term absences
- 60% decrease in behavioral incidents
- 20% increase in grades
- 100 paid internships
- 75 student jobs
- 3 college tours
- 30 field trips
- 30 kids inactive from street gangs
- 15 community service projects
- 50 guns off the streets
- 319 promoted to the next grade
- 100 high school graduates
- 15 enrolled and attending college
- 5 college graduates
- 2 married with families
- 6 business owners
- 120 children connected to primary care physicians
- 120 children diagnosed and treated for mental trauma.

Future Success Defined

Success for me is simple. Ask kids what they want. Ask them what they're interested in and build systems around exactly that. When you do that, you not only have their interest, but you keep them interested. My work focuses on currently behaviorally challenged future leaders. My brand has a proven measure of success. Therefore, I would like to see bipartisan, universal, mission-driven, quality investments made for education. This, coupled with communities of color uniting to hold professional athletes, entertainers, and corporations more socially and fiduciarily responsible for the education of those who pay them: our kids.

Gang Diversion, Reentry And Absent Fathers Intervention Clinical Services (GRAAFICS, 501c3) www.graafics.org	The Collaborative For Better Urban Health, LLC www.BetterUrbanhealth.com
[QR code and photo]	[QR code and photo]
FREE OFFER: $500.00 off your first 30 student, in-class, student workshop.	FREE OFFER: $100.00 off your first staff professional development training.
CONTACT To contact Kai Smith regarding inquiries related to his public school's behavior management program, please use: GRAAFICS.Program@gmail.com	CONTACT To contact Kai Smith regarding inquiries related to his children's mental health system, please use: BetterUrbanHealth@gmail.com

SOCIAL MEDIA

Please be advised, because 'GRAAFICS' and 'Better Urban Health' are two totally different companies, each has their own social media accounts. Please scan the QR Codes to gain access to the respective contacts for each company.

Erum Manzoor

Empowering Businesses and Championing Women in STEM

A visionary leader with an unwavering passion for technology, Erum has a proven track record of transforming multi-billion-dollar enterprises through strategic technology implementation. A sought-after keynote speaker and a recognized leader in Women in Technology, Erum is an advocate for harnessing technology to drive business growth and positive societal impact.

Empowering Girls in STEM Education: A Revolution in Progress
By Erum Manzoor

Having spent my career in corporate America, I've witnessed firsthand the transformative power of technology and its impact on society, particularly on women's leadership. I hold a deep respect for education and its role in shaping individuals.

My journey through various roles, including SVP for Retail Technology and Enterprise Architect, Partner at Strategic leadership practice, has provided me with a unique perspective on the intersection of technology, education, and women's leadership. I've seen how technology, when harnessed effectively, can break down barriers, create opportunities, and empower women to reach their full potential.

However, I also recognize that the foundation for women's leadership lies in education, particularly in STEM fields. Early exposure to STEM education instills confidence, problem-solving skills, and a passion for innovation, laying the groundwork for future success in technology and beyond.

Corporate sector, with its vast resources and global reach, can play a pivotal role in promoting STEM education for girls. By investing in STEM education initiatives, companies can attract and nurture a diverse pipeline of female talent, fostering a generation of women leaders equipped with the skills and knowledge to drive innovation and reshape the corporate landscape.

My commitment to STEM education begins from the belief that it can serve as a powerful catalyst for change, empowering women through technology and education. By advocating for STEM education, promoting inclusive workplaces, and leveraging technology to break down barriers, we can create a more equitable and prosperous future for all.

Therefore, I remain steadfast in my dedication to STEM, not merely as a career path but as a platform for driving positive change. I believe that by harnessing the power of technology and fostering a culture of education and inclusion, we can empower women to take their rightful place as leaders, innovators, and changemakers in the world.

The Ed Matadores mission resonates deeply with my endeavors. It is indispensable that we reshape the educational landscape to ensure equity, diversity, and inclusion. Bridging the gender gap in STEM is not just a matter of social justice but an imperative to unlock the full potential of our future leaders and innovators.

Bridging the Divide: The Importance of Women in STEM

STEM, or science, technology, engineering, and mathematics, is a rapidly growing field with a wide range of job opportunities. However, women are still underrepresented in STEM careers. According to the National Science Foundation, women make up only 28% of the workforce in science and engineering occupations.

There are many reasons why STEM education is important for girls. First, it provides them with the skills and knowledge they need to succeed in a variety of high-paying, in-demand jobs. STEM fields are also at the forefront of innovation, and girls who pursue STEM careers can make a real difference in the world.

Second, STEM education can help girls develop important problem-solving and critical thinking skills. STEM subjects teach girls how to think logically, solve complex problems, and come up with creative solutions. These skills are essential for success in all areas of life, not just in STEM careers.

Third, STEM education can help girls build confidence and self-esteem. When girls succeed in STEM subjects, they learn that they are capable of anything they set their minds to. This can lead to a lifetime of success and achievement.

There are many ways to encourage more girls to pursue STEM careers. One important step is to expose girls to STEM education early on. This can be done through extracurricular activities, such as STEM clubs and camps, as well as through in-school programs. It is also important to provide girls with role models in STEM fields. This can help girls see that STEM careers are accessible to them and that they can be successful in these fields.

Here are some specific things that parents, teachers, and other mentors can do to encourage girls to pursue STEM careers:
- Expose girls to STEM early and often. This can be done through books, toys, games, and activities that focus on science, technology, engineering, and math.
- Encourage girls to ask questions and explore their interests. Don't be afraid to let them experiment and try new things.
- Provide girls with opportunities to learn about STEM careers. This can be done through field trips, job shadowing, and mentorship programs.
- Challenge stereotypes and misconceptions about STEM fields. Let girls know that anyone can succeed in STEM, regardless of their gender.

Overcoming Roadblocks and Empowering Women: My Passion for STEM

In the intricate maze of the engineering world. My journey was not without its challenges, but it was fueled by an unwavering passion for innovation and a deep-seated desire to empower other women to pursue their STEM aspirations.

From my early days as an engineer, I was captivated by the intricate workings of the physical world, the harmonious interplay of science and technology. However, as I ventured deeper into the field, I found myself surrounded by a predominantly male workforce, a landscape that often felt alien and unwelcoming.

Despite these initial hurdles, I refused to be deterred. I immersed myself in my studies, devouring every morsel of knowledge I could find. I sought mentorship from experienced engineers, eagerly absorbing their wisdom and expertise. And I never ceased to question, to challenge, and to seek out new perspectives, determined to prove my worth.

As my confidence grew, so did my resolve to advocate for other women in STEM. I became a vocal supporter of diversity initiatives, actively mentoring young girls and encouraging them to embrace their passion for science and technology. I organized workshops and seminars, creating spaces where women could connect, share experiences, and foster a sense of community.

Over the years, I witnessed a remarkable shift in the landscape of the engineering field. Women's voices grew louder, their contributions more visible, their presence more undeniable.

My journey as a female engineer has been an odyssey of resilience, determination, and unwavering belief in the power of representation. It has been a privilege to witness firsthand the transformative impact of diversity and inclusion in STEM fields. And it has been an honor to play a small part in empowering the next generation of female engineers to navigate the labyrinth and leave their indelible mark on the world.

Studies consistently highlighted the importance of early exposure to STEM, particularly for girls, as a means to address gender disparities in STEM fields. We decided to provide opportunities for girls to explore and excel in STEM, breaking down the barriers that had held them back. Our initiative involved various components, including tailored STEM courses, mentorship programs, and community engagement. We experimented with different approaches, including modifying curriculum content and emphasizing female role models in STEM. Stakeholders, including teachers, parents, and students, were actively involved in the initiative. We presented it as a collective effort to empower our girls and create a more equitable learning environment.

Fostering a Collaborative Ecosystem for STEM education

To enable others to implement similar initiatives more easily, systemic changes are imperative. Firstly, educational institutions must adopt a proactive approach to address the gender gap in STEM. This includes implementing comprehensive, research-backed programs and providing professional development for educators to create inclusive classrooms.

Secondly, collaboration among schools, communities, and industry partners is vital. Initiatives like ours can benefit from shared resources, mentorship networks, and exposure to real-world STEM applications. Lastly, it is crucial to celebrate and amplify success stories to inspire more girls to pursue STEM education and careers.

In conclusion, the journey to empower girls in STEM education is ongoing, but the progress is evident. By revolutionizing our educational system, we can pave the way for a more equitable and innovative future where every girl can thrive in STEM. It is not just a mission; it's a societal imperative that we must all champion. Together we can make a difference!

Some of my headlines:
- Fostering a Future of Inclusive Innovation: Empowering Women in STEM Education.
- Championing Systemic Change for Gender Equity and STEM Education.
- Collaboration, Celebration, and Empowerment: Driving value for

ED. Matadores

Change in STEM Education
- Paving the Way for Future Generations: Embracing STEM Despite the Challenges for Women
- Breaking Barriers and Inspiring Others: My Journey as a Female Engineer Overcoming Roadblocks and Empowering Women: My Passion for STEM

Linktree:
https://linktr.ee/erum1_manzoor

www.linkedin.com/in/erummanzoorsvp

Insta: @erumscribbles01

X: erumscribbles

https://blinq.me/kGmXnFWlCtee?bs=db

Mary L. Jones

Mary L. Jones currently resides in Chicago, IL, and is a Mother of 1 son, Karim, married to Jonna; Grandmother to 22 and 8-year-old grandsons and a 9-year-old daughter. Mary has practiced educating Chicago residents in the area of the practical application of strategies that support housing retention, with a focus on financial literacy. AGORA Community Services, a HUD-Certified Housing Advising Agency, was created out of a need to address the systemic problem of homelessness that can be avoided by understanding the importance of financial literacy education. Mary's passion is to ensure that all who seek to understand how to provide and retain affordable housing for their family, have access to it before their housing situation reaches a critical level and faces homelessness. In 2011, AGORA became a Housing Advising Affiliate under HOMEFREE-USA, a HUD National Housing Intermediary. In 2023, HOMEFREE-USA National Housing Network was awarded President Joseph R Biden's Presidential Lifetime Achievement Award for Community Services. Mary has provided communities with education and resources to help families understand what is critical to being able to obtain and retain housing.

SHATTERED FOUNDATIONS
Linked to Youth Homelessness
TRUTHS // Youths, Financial Literacy, and Homelessness
By Mary L. Jones

To effectively address the elements missing in our society that lead to systemic homelessness, we must go back to the Foundation(s) where it originates. When a child believes his/her family is at risk of losing their housing and possibly they are already homeless, the child can no longer think about learning. They then grow up, and the cycle continues.

Their attention is ONLY on {1} how they maybe can help; {2} the feeling that there is nothing that they can do; {3} it is no longer a reason to study; all of the above can lead to deep depression. The concern: What has caused such a disconnect within the community, which also impacts our homeless children?

Cause: The family/community has fostered an ability to ignore that the child is affected by the prospect of being or becoming homeless. No support is given to the children in the community. It appears that it is believed that the child will be alright. Or, it will be that the possibility of any effect on the child is not even addressed by the family or community.

Cause: Not understanding the true definition of homelessness.
— The definition of homelessness. The definition: "A Fixed, Safe, Affordable, and Adequate nighttime residence". It is hard to collect data on youths affected by a crisis such as COVID-19 and other crises before COVID-19 if the data does not exist for ALL of our youths.

Here are some facts:
1) Illinois schools only collect data on homeless children under the age of 6 who are from Head Start Pl programs;
2) data does not include children who experience homelessness during the summer or when schools are closed and who have been forced to live with family or friends, which is usually cramped and sometimes not safe;
3) there is a stigma to being quote "at risk" of homelessness and actually homeless;
4) school personnel may be confused about what is actually homelessness; for example, if the child is living with a family member, there is usually no further concern on the part of the school and personnel, they feel they have somewhere to stay. The issue is that it's usually very temporary.

The Department of Health and Human Services estimates that we are actively able to count using the data collected. These numbers represent only 10% of the childhood homeless population. Also, it means that 90% are slipping through the cracks and experiencing homelessness with little to no assistance because they do not know where to go for assistance.

In 2020, they showed that 122,494 students ages 25 to 34 are homeless representing (20.8%); 17,646 represent students under the age of 12 approx. 14% approx. 14% of the student population. This data very clearly does not capture the true magnitude of youth homelessness.

"The Village Concept"

The foundation is family and the community which we will call the "Village Concept". Let's talk about the foundation of a village. The village is the composition of families, businesses, and community organizations and starts to provide services. If the village consists of these elements, it is important that they work together. There are many ways to work together, but we must start with the one thing we all have in common: Affordable housing - housing to shelter our families as well as a place for our stuff-- stuff that is important to us. Let's focus on the first issue with accomplishing affordable housing - thoroughly understanding affordable housing.

There are two components:

(1) Affordable housing: Definition A--available housing priced to match the needs and financial makeup of the residents in the village. This supports generational prosperity both in the community and in the families because they're able to plan through saving. If housing is not affordable and all monies are going towards housing, it becomes a great challenge to save. If you can't save, it becomes a greater challenge to sustain housing;

(2) Individual responsibility to know what your financial capacity is at any given time. This is important because every decision that we make can affect our ability to obtain and retain the housing that we need and/or desire. The purchase of any item above your means will cause future issues or concerns. When you add a good understanding of how to create a budget and a favorable credit score, you now have the basic formula for success and prosperity in many areas of your life including educational opportunities.

Generational Beliefs Impacts

Let's talk a little more about the foundation. If we think about generations, we have to understand that leaving tangible things such as houses, boats, and cars without leaving the financial literacy strategies, this will prevent us from being able to leave a legacy to our family or community.

When we teach financial literacy, we must reteach the whole family. When we also think about family foundations, we think about the community as family as well. There was a time when the village raised the children in the village -- Getting on a path to restore that is an integral part of restoring family and community. I do not want to leave anyone behind – for example: When a group of settlers came into a piece of land they felt would be a great place to raise their family and prosper, they immediately came together and built one large building which provided housing for everyone who was in need of immediate shelter. When that structure was close to completion, they started on the community needs, law structure to govern themselves, and worship/communication/food/clothing. Then, the attention was turned to building smaller homes; everyone participated in the building of each of those homes. One family moved out and into a home as it was built.

What does that say about today?

We barely know our neighbors; it feels strange to even speak to our neighbors, and sometimes there is fear. Because of the advancement of technology and other factors such as the economic and housing crisis, we now are living separately within our families and communities. It truly takes a family to raise a child, and it takes families that function as a village to build and restore and maintain a prosperous community. When a community functions as a village, our youths are educated in ALL areas of the community. The youths receive guidance and structure not only from their family but also from every aspect of their community. Homelessness can be eradicated when we stop the bleeding and educate our youths early on what is required to ensure housing retention, as they will one day be required to do so.

"I'm Just Saying..."

The Solution: When activated, we can begin to stop the bleeding in our society concerning housing and have a steady stream of new renters and homebuyers who are well-informed. Basically, they learn that they have access to housing agencies who will listen to them, educate them, and help them to reach their goal of housing sustainability for their family. First, we must address the family problem, which is the stigma about eviction and foreclosure that flows to the youths in the family. This has been ignored for many, many years. Our children see more than we believe and understand more than we believe they do. With the emergence of the 2008 Housing and Economic Crisis, followed by another one, and on top of that, before adequate restoration was achieved, COVID-19 hit the whole world, and many others became homeless, and many unknown challenges would follow. The family can show in their daily handling of a crisis strategies like looking for what "they" can do to resolve the issue -- then their children will also use that strategy, especially if it is shown to work!

"I'm Just Saying…"

There is governmental help, local community help, and family member help that may be considered; however, there is nothing to link self-help with timely and focused guidance. The family and community can restore their village with HUD-Certified Housing Advisers supported by HUD Housing and Urban Development; HomeFree-USA, a National Intermediary and local Partners/Investors for the community like Wells Fargo, PNC Bank, CIBC Bank, and Bank of America; Associated Bank and real estate brokers such as Exit Realty, Century 21, and RE/MAX. The Housing Counseling industry has been working hard to ensure that the FREE services offered are for the whole family; as mindsets are being developed, we believe that they must begin at the age of 15 or earlier depending on the youth. It is easier to develop a mindset at a young age than it is to reset or change the mindset of an adult!

"I'm Just Saying…"

The schools must include in their curriculum or in their Detention information that is going on in the community so that the youth will find the hope they need to concentrate on their schoolwork instead if they are going to have to sleep in the car again or at a residence that is not peaceful.

Why does our School Detention have to be a totally negative experience? It can be designed to uncover many problems that caused the Detention Assignment in the first place. Our youths are very smart, and with this information, they will instinctively begin to use it in as many areas of their lives as they can. The youths have been known to take information home and introduce it to their family. If children must go through a process of eviction and/or foreclosure, they should have some level of knowledge and understanding about what their family is going through– most are in the dark and scared. All that they are aware of is that something has uprooted their whole life. There should be a support system that is available to our youths in the schools, in the church, and in community organizations that do not avoid discussions about homelessness but deal with it on the appropriate level. They are no longer left in complete darkness about their housing. It is now more of a problem-solving situation to them, and the result can be a change in mindset!

"I'm Just Saying…"

Author:
Mary L Jones, Executive Director
AGORA HUD-Certified Housing Advising Agency

CONTACT AGORA:
Family and Community are very important elements to our future generations. By ensuring that our children receive every opportunity to grow, learn, and make healthy decisions, the results will be stronger families and communities that prosper from generation to generation. We must prepare our children with the proper mindsets about housing. If you would like more information on the services that we offer, use the below QR Code to speak with an AGORA Housing Adviser.

Instagram:

Facebook: https://www.facebook.com/profile.php?id=100063673563378

Dr. Emily R. Van Dyke

Dr. Emily R. Van Dyke (Siksika, Armenian, Irish, and Jewish) is a Biology Teacher, Independent College Counselor, writer, photographer, and advocate for high-quality education and health. She is an author on seven peer-reviewed articles regarding cancer care access and availability among American Indian/Alaska Native populations and enhancing health equity through responsible research practices. She is the founder of Pacific Northwest College Pathways, Immediate Past President of Native American Alumni of Harvard University, Children's Alliance Executive Committee and Public Policy Council Member, Harvard Club of Seattle Board leader, Seattle Harvard School of Public Health Chapter President, and is excellent at over-committing herself to causes in which she is passionate. She sees unlimited potential in her students and seeks to help them optimize their educational journeys through inquiring within themselves for what they really know about future potential college majors and resultant career pursuits. She received Harvard Alumni Association's Clubs & SIGs Outstanding Alumni Community Award as Native American Alumni of Harvard University (NAAHU) President in 2022 and NAAHU's Fire Keeper Award in 2020. She is dedicated to organizing and delivering excellent college counseling, biological instruction, and to longitudinal collaboration with a diverse array of stakeholders through her nineteen years of leadership roles on five boards.

Confronting The High School Academic Arms Race & Confronting The Potential Chilling Effect On College Campus Diversity In The Post-Affirmative Action Era
By Dr. Emily R. Van Dyke

As an Independent College Counselor, my main catchment area includes Seattle, Mercer Island, Issaquah, and Lake Washington School Districts. Established in the Fall of 2018 as a STEM and SAT/ACT tutoring business offering individually tailored one-on-one sessions, my business was rebranded in February 2021 as Pacific Northwest College Pathways. A retiring colleague graciously invited me to take on some of her Mercer Island-based college counseling clientele. Since I had guided multiple tutees (students) and mentees successfully through their college application process over the previous twelve years and since I had served throughout those years as a Harvard alumni interviewer, the transition to focusing on academic and college advising was a natural fit. I prioritize identifying students' intellectual and extracurricular passions, knowledge gaps, and family stressors and facilitating a calm learning environment to optimize the college application process and subject comprehension.

While I still enjoy tutoring students as they prepare to take their SAT/ACT exams, I assure them that these exams are not a robust indicator of future college or career success. In addition, SAT/ACT math topics remain out of step with most high school curricula: much of the math content is taught two years before the standard timing for SAT/ACT testing of that content. Meanwhile, for students whose parents did not attend college or attended college in another country, it is important to put these flawed metrics in perspective. Standardized test preparation time, tutoring, and resources for students who work time-consuming summer or school-year jobs to help their families get by will simply not be the same as for students who regularly receive carefully tailored guidance from tutors or test centers. Over 80% of colleges and universities have made a considerable step toward rebalancing the importance of these non-aptitude tests by remaining test-optional as of the 2022-2023 admissions cycle (Nietzel, 2022).

Dealing with Student Burn-Out

I have worked with many students prematurely burnt out by the ongoing academic arms race toward ever more AP classes and exams and by the too-common pre-COVID pressure to optimize superscores by taking the SAT and/or ACT five or six times. I gravitated to a radical model as a school-based college counselor. I sought an educational model that could offer teens a psychologically safe route through high school while yielding competitive results in college admissions. I found this philosophy at Woodinville Montessori School, which offers standard and honors courses but no AP options and places minimal emphasis on standardized test preparation or results. This Montessori high school is the only such school in the Pacific Northwest and remains significant: the school graduated four in the Class of 2022 and eight in the Class of 2023. Yet in the last days of August 2023, WMS Class of 2023 students moved to and matriculated at highly selective colleges and universities, including one Ivy League, one top tier public research university, a renowned art school, and two top tier engineering programs. Though the *n* of this uncontrolled case study is tiny, these results suggest that pushing for ever more AP courses is not the only path to admission to selective colleges.

Students who have the access privilege of longitudinal one-on-one support from an independent college counselor or have access to the rare school-based counselor who can provide individualized attention such that students receive the iterative and tailored equivalent of independent college counseling, as I provided at Woodinville Montessori School, have an undeniable advantage over the vast majority of public high school, first generation, and even many private school students. Most college counselors carry a student caseload of anywhere from 150-450 students each. Especially problematic during COVID remote schooling, schools must often reassign students based on changing staffing and enrollment. It is far too common for critical advice and counselor letters to be based on limited mutual knowledge and understanding between student and counselor.

Creation of NAAHU-Natives at Harvard College Mentorship Program

I passionately believe in the need to revolutionize the educational system and its success metrics. Success cannot be judged solely upon pushing students to take more AP classes and exams. Student stress and burnout too often accumulate when they reach college, so they cannot fully enjoy or benefit from the learning opportunities available. My colleagues and I have too often seen the psychological withdrawal and escalating stress that this academic arms race produces.

One route to providing that needed psychological support is offering mentorship and pipeline development programs in high school and college. As Native American Alumni of Harvard University (NAAHU)'s longest-serving President and during sixteen years on the NAAHU Board, I've striven to ensure that Native/Indigenous alumni and students have an active voice in national and international Harvard alumni communities. When Harvard students were given 3.5 days to vacate campus and find a way to store their belongings, we heard panic from BIPOC students who did not have sufficient funds to buy an urgent flight home and especially from American Indian, Alaska Native, and Hawaiian students whose home connectivity presented an ongoing roadblock to equal access to remote education as Harvard students. We mobilized quickly to create our NAAHU-Natives at Harvard College Mentorship Program so that students suddenly isolated at home could receive psychosocial and career support from Native/Indigenous alumni whose lived experience at Harvard had been similarly isolating and radically unlike the stereotypes associated with Harvard students.

For the over 90% of high school students who attend public school, whose administration and teachers cannot be radically responsive to each student's evolving academic and psychiatric needs, are such mentorship programs scalable? Will the Supreme Court verdict striking down affirmative action have a chilling effect on Diversity, Equity, Inclusion, and Belonging hires and admissions? The COVID pandemic taught us that K-12 and higher education institutions *can be* rapidly responsive given a strong enough impetus. Given the level of student disenchantment, burnout, and even rare suicides over college admissions pressures, surely we ought to have sufficient incentive to redress the academic arms race that tells students that more As and 5s in more APs are never enough. Though scaling back the intense pressure while remembering the social and emotional needs of students often impacted by distance learning will be a fraught endeavor at many competitive high schools, we can look to mentorship programs in the meantime to support BIPOC and LGBTQ+ students.

Modest Progress Towards Socioeconomic Diversity But More is Needed

Though Harvard and its peer institutions have made modest progress toward welcoming socioeconomic diversity, the assumptions remain on and off campus that the Harvard student is inevitably wealthy. In *The Privileged Poor,* Anthony Jack discussed the academic and psychological impacts of being the rare student in a given Ivy League milieu who worries about affording food during school breaks rather than even considering joining "peers" on ski breaks. When I first heard him speak in person about his research at a Harvard Club of Seattle Crimson Achievement Program event, his words brought me to silent tears of recognition and release since I had felt entirely alone as I quietly squirreled away oranges from the dining hall before its closure for winter and spring breaks. This socioeconomic invisibility for the "doubly disadvantaged" in Jack's parlance, borne by both non-Hispanic White and BIPOC students, can have huge consequences for a student's educational trajectory, alumni engagement, and lifespan.

High school counselors and college admissions staff might target these disparities in the future. Meanwhile, admissions advantages for the super-wealthy persist. As long as they do, attrition and alienation will be a risk for BIPOC, especially AI/AN/PI students whose lived realities are absent from the curriculum and poorly understood by peers. Harvard Economists Raj Chetty and David J. Deming and Brown's John N. Friedman published "Diversifying Society's Leaders? The Determinants and Causal Effects of Admission to Highly Selective Private Colleges" in July 2023, which revealed that children from families from the top 1% were 34% more likely to be admitted and that children from families in the top 1% are 2.2 times as likely to attend an Ivy-Plus college (Ivy League, Stanford, MIT, Duke, and Chicago) as those from middle-class families with comparable SAT/ACT scores based on data from 1999 to 2015 (Saul, 2023).

Far from the racial balancing that conservative Supreme Court justices feared, BIPOC admissions numbers had already declined for Harvard's Class of '27 – even before the Supreme Court overruled forty years of precedent with their SFFA v. Harvard (6-2) verdict (Amponsah, Haidar, & Staff Writers, 2023). It is critical to remind our high school students that colleges and universities still want a full and nuanced account of what matters to them. Whether their racial or ethnic background has been inspirational, challenging, or neutral, whether their race has illuminated and lifted them up, held them back, both at different times in their lives, or neither, we must ensure that students are aware that they are still permitted to share these narratives in college essays and to discuss relevant student activism in their activities lists. Students also need to know that "box checking" on the Common App is data that will likely not be seen by selective colleges, so if their lived experiences, perspectives, and potential contributions to their undergraduate class related to race and ethnicity are to be considered, they need to be reflected in prose like personal statements, supplemental essays, and/or activities list information. Dozens of colleges have updated their Common App supplemental essay prompts specifically to invite students to discuss how they envision contributing to continued diversity on campus (Knox,

2023). For instance, Sarah Lawrence College directly cites Chief Justice Roberts' decision. It prompts students to reflect on examples from their lives and to anticipate ways in which their college education may be impacted by this momentous Spring 2023 Supreme Court decision, in taking action to live up to their pre-decision promises, these colleges and universities mirror Justice Sotomayor's words.

Justice Sotomayor, in dissent, declared that "the pursuit of racial diversity will continue. Although the court has stripped out almost all uses of race in college admissions, universities can and should continue to use all available tools to meet society's needs for diversity in education. Despite the court's unjustified exercise of power, the opinion today will only highlight the court's impotence in the face of an America whose cries for equality resound."

Free Offer: Introductory 30 min College Counseling Session

Contact ME

Business website: https://pnwcollegepathways.com/

PNW College Pathways FB link:
https://www.facebook.com/PNWCollegePathways/

LinkedIn Profile: https://www.linkedin.com/in/emilyrvandyke

Instagram: PNW College Pathways (@pnwcollegepathways)

ED. Matadores

Casanova Green
Director of First Year Experience, Diversity, and Inclusion
Hocking College

Casanova Green is the Director of First Year Experience, Diversity, and Inclusion at Hocking College in Nelsonville, OH. He holds a BA in Language Arts Education from Ohio Northern University, an MFA in Creative Writing from Reinhardt University, and is pursuing a PhD in Rhetoric and Composition from Ohio University. He is an experienced high school and collegiate educator, a published poet and essayist, a recording artist, and a pastor.

Leveling The Playing Field:
An Introduction To Justice Pedagogy
By Casanova Green

Entering into the post-Secondary Arena

Hocking College is a two-year vocational and technical community college renowned for its Natural Resource and Nursing programs. Nestled in the Appalachian Foothills in southeastern Ohio, the college serves people from the region as well as from Ohio and other states and international students from places such as Jamaica and Botswana. We are also the first residential community college in Ohio, which, along with athletics, has drawn a large Black and Latino population. The area that surrounds the college has been hit hard by the effects of COVID-19, poverty, drug abuse, and limited educational experiences and opportunities. Athens County is one of the poorest counties in Ohio.

I started my time at Hocking as an adjunct English Instructor in October 2019. Although I taught my classes online, I held in-person office hours and got to know and connect with the faculty, staff, and students at Hocking. I even had former students that I taught in high school. I immediately felt connected to the college and knew that I wanted to be there on a continual basis. However, COVID-19 delayed those plans.

In June 2021, I was tasked with helping revamp the English curriculum along with other adjuncts and the sole full-time faculty member. There were a couple of meetings, but then everything stopped. I called the General Studies Program Manager in July 2021, and she frantically listed off what was going on.

"We are having some difficulty getting this course ready and aligned," she said. "We really need to reformat this course, but I know nothing about English."

I responded, "Honestly, you all need a Director of Composition."

She paused and took a deep breath. "We know, and we want it to be you."

In August 2021, I left my Graduate Assistantship at Ohio University and was hired full-time as the Journalism Program Manager. I had a week to create a new Composition I course. I reached out to Ohio University to use their Composition I framework as a foundation, and they graciously and quickly approved. That foundation helped create the current Composition I course at Hocking.

The Motivation Behind Justice Pedagogy

When people find out that I am working on my doctorate, they tend to ask, "So, Cas, what is your research focus for your PhD?"

I state calmly, "My focus is on composition pedagogy for marginalized groups with a focus on first-year composition courses."

Most of the time, I get a blank stare, and they change the subject. I get the occasional nod or "Wow. Okay." The responses I typically receive show a strong sense of confusion because people outside and within academia do not consider the needs of students who do not have an affluent or suburban upbringing and lack a lot of support and resources.

My passion for this topic was birthed during my tenure as a high school English teacher at two charter high schools in Columbus, OH. I had the opportunity to teach students from across the world who had amazing potential but felt like they could not write. I would shepherd them through creating poems, songs, and articles, which showed a mastery of these styles. However, they were discouraged because they had difficulty writing in Standard Academic English (SAE) and were degraded because of it. Being in the postsecondary space has shown me the wounds and damage this causes students even decades after they had high school English.

As I created the Composition course, I thought about how to make the course accessible to all students by honoring what they bring to the experience and using that to prepare them for real-world application and transfer of these ideas. A lot of students are not empowered to compose and communicate in all aspects of life because one person said they were deficient in one form of writing. Using what I learned and continue to glean from my Ph.D. work at Ohio University, I was affirmed and inspired to build a pedagogical framework to empower students to effectively communicate their story and message effectively.

The Strategy: Defining Justice Pedagogy

When people hear of the concept of justice, they think of retribution and punishment. The concept of justice is best described as balance or stasis—removing the barrier rather than accommodating it as best as possible. In our diversifying academic and professional worlds, we have to realize that the rules are changing. People are leveraging social media and composing for the web from older forms. Also, people are looking to hear and experience people who identify with them as they are in a way they understand.

The traditional composition classroom does not account for this. The focus is mainly on writing in more academic genres rather than giving students the ability to use real-world genres which connect to their career pursuits. Secondly, as Kermit Campbell notes in the article "There Goes the Neighborhood: Hip Hop Creepin' on a Come Up at the U," first-year composition courses tend to favor white, middle-class students. These students tend to speak and write in what is considered the standard because those around them model that linguistic register. Also, the classroom space focuses on SAE rather than engaging students where they are and embracing code-switching or code-meshing and giving validity to their linguistic experiences. Since white, middle-class students are steeped in the standard experience, they have an advantage to succeed in courses more than other groups.

The goal of Justice Pedagogy is to create balance in the writing classroom by providing students opportunities to compose traditional and nontraditional texts that employ real-world practices that will transfer to many aspects of their personal, professional, and academic lives and use their lived experiences and cultural experiences and competencies to influence and expand opportunities for students to compose in a professionalized mindset rather than an assimilative practice. Justice Pedagogy cannot be siloed in an imagined space. It is best employed in real-world situations and authentic tasks and in real audiences that matter to the student and the topic to promote high-road and low-road transfer of skills. This pedagogical model works to make the intentions of the Conference on College Composition and Communication's statement "Students Right to their Own Language" come alive: to validate students' linguistic experiences and heritages in the classroom and for teachers to model respect for the diversity students offer and affirm the student's right to use the languages of their discourse communities.

The Playbook: Enacting Justice Pedagogy

In creating the new Composition I course and eventually rebuilding the English department, I found four key concepts that ground the course and set a foundation for student success. The first one is understanding rhetoric and its strategic use. Most students see rhetoric as three things: ethos, logos, and pathos. Justice Pedagogy extends this foundation by adding a fourth rhetorical appeal, kairos, and extending the concept of rhetoric by focusing on the intentionality of text, design, and other areas. Students learn that rhetoric is everywhere, and everything has a message. I include examples including social media strategies, people's style of dress, music videos, and TED Talks to allow them to see how rhetoric moves beyond those three things.

The second is an understanding of genre and how it works with rhetoric to convey a message. As students prepare to enter the workforce, they must be versed in several genres of composing and writing to convey a message. The first thing I do is teach about genres and then explain that academic writing is a genre of writing rather than the only way to write. Genres are vital because they need to be able to determine the best genre and method to use depending on the rhetorical situation to effectively convey the desired message. This pillar empowers students to employ what they know or challenge themselves to convey the message effectively.

The third concept is multimodality. They learn how intentional design choices, or modes, work together to create a digestible message. They already do these things in their lives through social media, texting, and other creative outlets. However, they are unaware of how research and sourcing can happen outside of an essay. With a multimodal framework, students can use other options to convey their stance and research in ways that people can understand and engage with it. The last concept is process. Using a social cognitivist framework, we focus on writing as a process and a social act. Students learn or review the importance of the writing process and the need to have someone look at it and support them. The process is designed to create a space for mutual learning and alleviate issues as they arise.

Playing the Game: Implementation, Obstacles, and Outcomes

The course was initially implemented in August 2021. As usual, students were very nervous about the class until they saw what I was doing. The class is taught in eight weeks online and in-person. Using Understanding by Design, I was able to figure out how to put it together so it builds. Students have four major writing assignments: a literacy narrative, a rhetorical analysis, an annotated bibliography, and a persuasive research project. Each major writing assignment builds upon the last one. Students are highly encouraged to do multimodal projects.

There were two obstacles. First, it was the time constraint. Eight weeks is a hard schedule. I felt that I had to rush initially. As I continue teaching, things get easier. The other reason is that I am no longer leading the department. We have hired a great Director of Communications Lab working to carry things on and finish everything.

The results from the new class show that people are passing the course at higher rates than the old curriculum. Students feel safer in the spaces and are willing to seek help when they need it. One result that shocked me was that students who took the course with me were twice as likely to graduate from the college than anyone else.

Looking to the Future

In the field of rhetoric and composition, there must be a realization that change is needed, especially as we embrace the diversification of America. The mission of Ed. Matadores to revolutionize the field of teaching is vital, and Justice Pedagogy provides opportunities to do just that. We must move from a gatekeeping mindset in the writing classroom and classes that rely on written communication to a bridge-building mindset where students can apply and connect what they are learning to their life and professional experiences. As I always told my Composition students, "If you know the rules, you'll win the game."

Scan Here to Connect With Me	Scan here to have me at your next event.

ED. Matadores

INTERNATIONAL EDUCATION

Dr. Tadios Belay
President and CEO of the U.S. Africa Institute

Dr. Tadios Belay, President and CEO of U.S. Africa Institute, champions educational equity for marginalized students in the U.S. and Across Africa. Dr. Belay's advocacy and dedication extend to the United Nations, where he worked on the Global Compact for Migration, promoting educational and gender equity.

Dr. Tadios Belay attended the University of San Francisco School of Law, attended the prestigious Executive Education Program at the Harvard Kennedy School of Government, and completed his doctoral degree in Global Education and Policy at the University of Southern California (USC) where his research works focused on the intersection of global education, identity, culture and student achievement in predominantly White Colleges and Universities.

Promoting Diversity And Fostering Belonging: The Role Of Virtual Exchange To Support Historically Marginalized Students In U.S. Higher Education

By Dr. Tadios Belay

My name is Dr. Tadios Belay, President and CEO of the U.S. Africa Institute. My career has been marked by unwavering advocacy for educational equity and justice. I have made it my life's mission to work at the intersection of some of the most pressing issues in higher education today, particularly those impacting historically marginalized students in predominantly white institutions (PWIs). More than just ensuring these students access to tertiary education, my passion lies in creating an environment where they do not merely exist but truly belong, adding their unique experiences and perspectives to the vibrant tapestry of campus life. This commitment extends to my research realm, where I explore the lived experiences of these students at PWIs in-depth. My studies span a broad spectrum of factors affecting their educational journey, including cultural and identity development, campus climate, sense of belonging, faculty support, socioeconomic issues, and retention and completion rates.

Ed Matadores' mission deeply aligns with my own commitment to racial and educational equity, demonstrating our shared dedication to mitigating educational and racial disparities. Both Ed Matadores and I endorse the idea that education should enlighten and free individuals, not homogenize them. I value diversity not only in terms of race and ethnicity but also in thoughts, ideas, and perspectives. I concur with the need for a radical transformation in the current education system, advocating for an equity and racial justice approach. The current system often widens disparities, particularly for marginalized communities, an issue that must be urgently and effectively addressed. Ed Matadores' mission stands as a beacon in this endeavor.

This chapter outlines the U.S. Africa Institute's initiatives, which I lead to bolster diversity and foster a sense of belonging in higher education through virtual exchange programs. It examines the role of virtual exchange, challenges, research, and successes, serving as a rallying cry for a revolution in higher education. We strive to build a more inclusive, compassionate, and fair society, offering all students the opportunities they deserve.

Unveiling the Institutional Barriers to Address Educational Inequities

A closer examination reveals that Predominantly White Institutions (PWIs) often perpetuate systemic injustices and glaring disparities, particularly against historically marginalized students. This unfortunate reality forms a dismal backdrop to the experiences of these students, underscoring the immediate need for innovative solutions such as the implementation of virtual exchange programs. These programs need to be specifically designed to engage, target and include historically marginalized students in PWIs.

The hurdles faced by these students are deeply woven into the tapestry of these institutions. A plethora of obstacles, including deeply rooted institutional racism, a lack of supportive environments, an unsatisfactory campus climate, and a diminished sense of belonging, obstruct their educational journey. Each of these barriers stands as a stark testament to the extreme deficit of diversity and sense of belonging in PWIs, shaping an environment that is far from conducive to the nurturing and development of every student's growth and potential.

An exploration into these issues uncovers a clear and sobering image: the pathway to success for historically marginalized students in PWIs is often impeded by a range of factors. This reality further heightens the pressing need for change. Educational equality, a crucial building block of societal progress and advancement, can only be realized when these institutions actively confront these disparities. This requires promoting an inclusive, supportive environment that is conducive to the growth and potential of every student, particularly through the integration of comprehensive virtual exchange programs designed to support and include historically marginalized students.

Navigating the Turbulent Historical Landscape of Black Students in the U.S. Higher Education System

To appreciate the depth of these issues, it is vital to revisit the historical context of Black students' journey in American higher education— a journey fraught with exclusion and hardship. The entrance of Black students into these hallowed halls of learning wasn't until the 1830s, a time when the echoes of emancipation rang through the corridors of history. The 1960s saw a significant surge in the number of Black students, largely due to the enactment of the Civil Rights Act and Higher Education Act. This era symbolized hope and progression, but despite these strides, the journey remained arduous, marred by feelings of isolation, marginalization, and a lack of academic and emotional support.

Affirmative Action emerged as a beacon of hope in this grim landscape, a policy designed to redress these racial inequities and foster diversity in colleges and universities. However, the recent Supreme Court ruling against affirmative action presents a significant setback for diversity and a sense of belonging on college campuses. This decision poses an existential threat to the representation of historically marginalized students, exacerbating the challenges they face and highlighting the urgent need for alternative solutions.

Innovative Initiatives

Recognizing the magnitude and intricacies of these challenges, the U.S. Africa Institute embarked on implementing innovative initiatives. These initiatives focused primarily on fostering diversity and nurturing a sense of belonging. The creation of Virtual Exchange Programs, a groundbreaking approach towards learning, served as the cornerstone of these initiatives. Initially, this new venture began with a small pilot project, a small step towards a significant change. We learned from this experience, understanding and adapting to the unique challenges that surfaced during implementation.

One major obstacle was the limited technological infrastructure in underserved communities, a stark reminder of the disparities existing outside the confines of our campuses. Resistance from educators steeped in traditional teaching methods also posed a hurdle, pointing to the deeper roots of the problem. Moreover, student participation rates were lower than expected, reflecting the general apprehension toward change.

Determined to overcome these barriers, we formed strategic partnerships with tech companies, setting out to tackle the digital divide head-on. Simultaneously, we recognized the necessity for a paradigm shift among educators and launched faculty development programs. These programs aimed to educate educators about the benefits and methods of virtual and hybrid learning.

The results were heartening and rewarding. We observed a significant increase in enrollment from historically marginalized students. Academic performances improved, as measured by standard metrics, and students' engagement rates rose. Most importantly, we saw the development of an enhanced sense of belonging reported by many students. This positive feedback, coupled with improved learning outcomes, served to reinforce our belief in the potential of these innovative educational approaches.

Collaboration and Challenges

Collaboration is undeniably the cornerstone of any successful initiative aimed at fostering change on a grand scale. As we embarked on this transformative journey, it was evident that our efforts needed to be supplemented and enriched by the input, expertise, and backing of various stakeholders.

Working in tandem with higher learning institutions was crucial to the success of our mission. These partnerships provided us with critical insights into the structural and systemic barriers to diversity and inclusion prevalent within these spaces. Armed with this knowledge, we could fine-tune our initiatives to precisely target and dismantle these impediments, promoting an environment conducive to diversity, inclusion, and belonging.

Additionally, these collaborations brought forth opportunities to influence institutional policies and practices directly. We could advocate for amendments and reforms that prioritized diversity and inclusivity at the core of institutional operations. By working closely with these institutions, we managed to spark critical dialogues around inclusivity, gradually driving the wheels of change toward more diverse and representative student populations.

Engagement with policymakers was another essential facet of our collaborative strategy. Their influence and decision-making capabilities offered a channel to advocate for equitable educational policies on a broader, systemic scale. Through persistent dialogue and negotiation, we strived to bring the plight of historically marginalized students to the forefront of educational policy discussions.

However, the path to these accomplishments was not without its fair share of challenges. Perhaps the most significant was resistance to change, a universal obstacle when undertaking initiatives that challenge long-standing norms and practices. Many institutions displayed a reluctance to alter established practices and systems. Breaking down these barriers of resistance required persistent advocacy, demonstration of the benefits of diversity and inclusion, and the courage to confront established norms.

Another significant challenge was the institutionalization of diversity and inclusion practices across all levels of the university. Implementing such practices is one thing, but ensuring their pervasiveness and permanence within the institution is an entirely different, often more formidable task. Institutionalization demanded an overhaul of university culture and necessitated the full commitment of every faculty, staff, and student within the institution. Lastly, our initiatives, like many others with broad ambitions, were often curtailed by the lack of sufficient resources and funding. Forging new paths in the realm of higher education requires considerable financial investment. The scarcity of funds often limited the scope of our initiatives and constrained our ability to scale them effectively. Despite these challenges, our commitment to promoting diversity and fostering a sense of belonging in higher education remained undeterred. Each obstacle served as a learning opportunity, shaping our approach and strengthening our resolve to build a more inclusive and equitable higher education system.

Call for Systemic Change

The successful replication and implementation of such initiatives in other institutions necessitate profound and far-reaching systemic changes. There are multiple facets to this issue, and each one must be addressed diligently and comprehensively.

At the crux of these systemic changes is the urgent need to address the digital divide. This divide, characterized by disparities in access to information and communication technology, hampers students from different backgrounds, preventing them from accessing quality technological infrastructure. This lack of access invariably creates a chasm in educational opportunities, particularly apparent in this digital age where learning increasingly leverages technology. Thus, a concerted effort is required to bridge this divide, investing in infrastructural improvements and promoting digital literacy in underserved communities. This will ensure that all students, regardless of their socioeconomic backgrounds, can avail themselves of the technological resources necessary for contemporary learning.

Another crucial change lies in the pedagogical approach to education. The traditional models, often rigid and inflexible, fail to cater to the diverse learning needs and styles of students. Instead, a shift towards flexible, inclusive, and learner-centric approaches is necessary. These approaches should accommodate the unique backgrounds and learning styles of each student, treating diversity as a resource rather than a challenge. Such a transformation would involve restructuring curricula, teaching methodologies, and assessment practices, embedding principles of equity and inclusion at their very core.

Finally, the fostering of a culture of inclusivity and belonging within educational institutions is a critical component of systemic change. This calls for more than just the mere acceptance of diversity. It demands a holistic transformation of our institutions into safe and nurturing spaces for all students. This involves acknowledging and validating the identities, experiences, and contributions of every student as an essential aspect of the educational environment. It also necessitates the provision of necessary support, be it academic, emotional, or social, to help students navigate the complexities of higher education. Implementing such support systems involves active efforts from faculty, staff, and administrators to promote an environment of understanding, empathy, and mutual respect. In essence, the systemic changes needed for promoting diversity and fostering a sense of belonging in higher education are multifaceted. Addressing the digital divide, fostering a paradigm shift in education, and creating a culture of inclusivity and belonging are necessary steps toward this goal. The collective effort to implement these changes will set the stage for an educational environment where every student has an equal opportunity to thrive.

A Revolutionary Call for Equity and Justice in U.S. Higher Education

In conclusion, to truly revolutionize the educational system, we must view it through lenses of equity and racial justice. By embracing innovative solutions and transformations, we can create a more diverse, inclusive, and just educational landscape. A paradigm shift in our approach to education, especially for historically marginalized students, is not just a suggestion - it is a call for a revolution. It is in heeding this call that we can hope to shape a future of education that acknowledges, respects, and values the diversity and richness of all its participants—a future that fosters belonging and inspires growth for all.

Contact Dr. Radios Belay

Free Offer

As a token of appreciation for engaging with my book chapter, I would like to offer my readers to download my research paper, "Advancing Black Identity and Culture in Predominantly White Colleges and Universities: A Promising Practice Study," to provide actionable strategies and best practices that college administrators, educators, and students can implement to create a more inclusive and supportive environment and promote diversity and fostering belonging on college campuses. The research paper provides a comprehensive exploration of the experiences of Black students in predominantly white institutions, offering valuable insights and a nuanced understanding of the challenges they may face. I want my readers to take action to foster meaningful dialogues on diversity, inclusion, and the experiences of historically marginalized students. I also encourage my readers to engage stakeholders and college administrators to translate insights from my research into tangible actions, creating a lasting impact on the academic and social experiences of Black students in higher education.

Dr. Heinrich Heinrichs
africrops! GmbH, CEO and Founder

Dr. Heinrich Heinrichs is a scientist and education expert who has been working worldwide for the last 30 years with growing responsibilities. He has worked with and within Education Ministries in various countries and supported the development of education and training policies. In 2013 he founded africrops!, a company that combines trading and development with Africa. The company follows the philosophy, "Don't ask what Africa needs, but what Africa has that the world needs!".

During the last years, his emphasis has been on combining vocational training systems with entrepreneurial elements. The focus is on organic farming and other areas related to sustainable development strategies.

Filling The Social Gap With H3 - Head, Hand, And Heart: Competency Based Vocational Training The africrops! Way
By Dr. Heinrich Heinrichs

Introduction and Context

africrops! GmbH is a company based in Berlin that works with African partners by developing competencies to become successful in local, regional, and international markets. This includes quality aspects in the production process and entrepreneurship skills. The production follows organic principles with the respective certification for the international markets.

Working for the last 20 years with Ministries of Education in various African countries, it became clear that there is a growing number of young people who don't finish school or don't continue with their education after school. To fill this gap, vocational training is a very suitable system that leads to a formal qualification and getting these young people back into the system.

The DACH-countries (Germany, Austria, and Switzerland) have very strong vocational training systems. They are based on a dual principle: 4 days a week the trainee works as an apprentice in a company and 1 day per week he/she must go to a vocational training school. While this system works well in the above-mentioned countries, copying it in other countries was never successful. This system has grown over the centuries, and a key feature is that a company that offers apprenticeships needs specially trained people, i.e. the so-called "Meister" for artisan companies. To establish such a system from scratch is not really sensible and would need an effort that is out of any proportions.

A Namibian organization, Komeho Development Agency asked africrops! to develop a vocational training system for a training farm in rural Namibia. The Namibia Training Authority and various donors had supplied the infrastructure, tools, boarding facilities, etc.

Problem - Solution Identification

While it is rather not sensible to adopt the vocational training system from the DACH countries to another country, there are some features that can be translated into a new context:
- Focusing on Competency rather than only on knowledge
- Creating a training environment that comes close to real professional life rather than a school

Competency-based education and training

Namibia has done large steps in creating world-class curricula during the last 20 years. In an Education and Training Sector Improvement Programme (ETSIP) the whole sector was reformed to overcome the social divide of the past, i.e. the racial divide due to Apartheid policies. For this purpose, international experts were involved. The new education and training policies follow the principle of competency-based education and training.

However, when talking about competency, the implementation side is critical. Our definition of competency relates to three components: knowledge (head), skills (hands), and values and attitudes (heart). We call it H3.

Fig. 1: Trainees collaborate preparing their fields for organically grown crops.

When implementing the H3 approach, it also has an impact on the assessment strategy. While knowledge is rather easy to assess through written or oral tests ("the trainee has discovered root-knot nematodes in Swiss chart"), skills are related to the actual doing ("Mathilda is the best welder"). For the assessment of the attitude, other techniques like self- and peer assessment play an important role ("My patch looks so nice because of commitment to get up early in the morning and remove the caterpillars", "I like the way she is treating her vegetable patch!"). Attitude is to a large extent created through role models. The trainers play a crucial role here.

Creating a training environment close to reality

We saw that many vocational training centers are dysfunctional. Trainees spent most of their time in a classroom, and once they successfully completed the training with a qualification, the industry found them lacking the skills to fulfill their jobs. This detachment from real work life led us to distinguish between education and vocational training: Education is for life; vocational training is to make a living!

Of course, we do not deny the close relationship between the two and the overlapping in certain aspects.

Therefore, we created a training environment that to a certain extent simulates the work environment of a job.
- Everybody has his/her own little patch where vegetables are grown.
- The training includes a module on entrepreneurship in agriculture.
- While the produce of the farm is integrated into the daily diet, the surplus is sold to the community close to the training farm.
- After one year of training the trainees are sent for job attachment at commercial farms.

Fig. 2: Packing the onions produced to be sold on the local farmers market.

One important element of the dual training in German-speaking countries is that the trainees work four days per week in an accredited company and learn one day per week in a vocational training school.

In other words: 80% of the time trainees spent in the field and 20% in the classroom. This principle was used, however, in a different way: Generally, 1.5 hours (2 periods) per day were spent in the classroom; 6 hours were spent in the field. This was handled flexibly. In the meantime this approach was adapted to other countries as well, however always considering the special situation in a particular country. In every country, vocational education and training are organized differently.

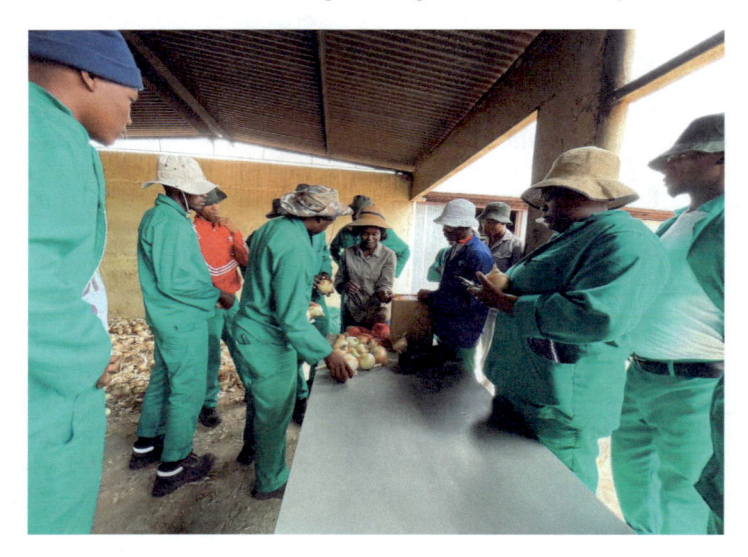

Lessons learned and best practices

Potent Partner:
The partner structures need an appropriate infrastructure and stakeholders that are willing to support new ways of developing young people. The private sector, foundations, and NGOs play a vital role in making it successful. The support of community members makes it strong.

Close collaboration with Governmental structures:
The training should be in line with governmental policies from the very beginning. This ensures acceptance and support through these public players and access to curricula, standards, tools etc., and financial support, which makes it sustainable.

Focus on competencies rather than knowledge:
H3 works! Modern education and training systems define competencies. However, to implement them, very well-trained and experienced trainers are vital! These should also have a background in the respective industry rather than only in a training setting. Vocational trainers rarely have an extensive educational background. With the Head – Hand – Heart approach, competency is easy to understand and to implement.

Use standards and curricula that are already in place:
Often the focus is on curricula and standards; however, our experience has shown that the implementation is key, i.e., how a curriculum is implemented and how relevant a certain content is trained. Re-writing standards and curricula might be necessary sometimes. Still, the way of implementation is often underestimated: Don't reinvent the wheel but rather find out new ways on how to use them!

Offer national qualifications:
Vocational training has the potential to get school dropouts back into the system. Furthermore, successful trainees have an opportunity to get a qualification without going to colleges or universities with extremely high tuition fees. Therefore, vocational training offers the opportunity to bridge the gap between the social disparities.

Go organic:
Organic food is in growing demand. Therefore, organic farming provides the opportunity to become a successful member of society. High-quality standardized training aiming on competency rather than merely knowledge will make the difference. Often, organic farming is self-taught. Quality training can make sure that highly qualified people will enter the quality job market!

Conclusion:
To effectively prepare trainees for real-life work environments and situations, it is sensible, perhaps even imperative to place them in these practical settings. The dual approach advocated by German-speaking countries has a proven track record of doing this successfully. While many lessons can be learnt from this, it is our experience that the principles cannot be applied 1:1 in other countries. They must be adapted to the local environment to reflect local business and educational structures, as well as market demands – this is after all the environment for which they are being prepared.

Fig. 3: Proud team on their training farm in the Kalahari Desert of Namibia.

Free Offer:
The German writer Erich Kästner said "*Es gibt nichts Gutes, außer man tut es*" (nothing is good, unless you do it!). Please watch the documentary showing how H3 works in Namibia!

https://www.youtube.com/watch?v=bqZRTPKqmt8

Contact Heinrich Heinrichs

https://www.linkedin.com/in/heinrich-heinrichs-phd-60361129/

ED. Matadores

NEUROSEMANTICS

Louise Debreczeny, Ed.D.
CEO INSL LLC

Dr. Louise Debreczeny, the dynamic Owner/CEO of the Institute for Neurosemantic and Sociocognitive Learning (INSL LLC), is a vanguard in the sphere of educational innovation. Possessing a profound academic background with an Ed.D. specializing in Neuroeducation from the University of Portland, she seamlessly integrates a rich and varied tapestry of life experiences into her educational philosophy. Through INSL LLC, Lou champions an educational revolution, harmonizing education with the intrinsic learning patterns of individuals and fostering a society that celebrates the full spectrum of human learning and creativity.

Drawing: The Eighth Literacy
By Louise Debreczeny, Ed.D.

When the idea of drawing is mentioned, most people immediately think of art, which of course, is logical. But drawing can also be used to represent your thinking in the form of stick figures without worrying if it is art or not. This chapter is about drawing, the eighth literacy, and how it is the missing element in literacy instruction, and why it is important to add in this missing element. To put drawing's importance into perspective, we need to examine all eight of the processes of literacy (listen/speak/read/write/think/calculate/view/draw), and how drawing fits into that system of processes.

Typically, in schools, teachers emphasize seven of the eight processes of literacy, and the eighth process, drawing, is left out. Cooper (2006) in *Literacy: Helping Children Construct Meaning* describes how to use seven processes to help learners develop literacy. These seven processes are reading, writing, speaking, listening, thinking, calculating and viewing. The one that is left out is drawing.

How do we know that drawing is the missing process? We can match up the processes in pairs and look at how in each pair one activity is receptive and the other is expressive. So, reading and writing go together, with writing as the expressive process and reading the receptive process. Speaking and listening match up in a similar way with speaking being expressive and listening receptive. Thinking and calculating also have an expressive and receptive nature. Then that leaves viewing all by itself with no expressive piece to pair up with it. In thinking about what might pair up with viewing, we have to look at what expressive process must be used to create something another person can view. So, there must be some kind of process to project one's ideas so that another person can view them. We have multiple processes available to us to create projections, but we cannot simply ask learners at school to create a video to represent their thinking until the learner is old enough to learn video production and only then if the technology to make such a creation is available. What can learners do to project their thinking that is readily available and easy for children to do? The answer is stick-figure drawing.

The Eight Processes of Literacy

Receptive processes of literacy	Expressive processes of literacy
Listen	Speak
View	Draw
Think	Calculate
Read	Write

So, we can see that drawing does fit in with the other processes of literacy, but why is it so important to add it into our literacy programs? For students with visual motor learning systems, drawing is an essential element of learning. In my practice I have worked with a large number of students who have visual motor learning systems who had fallen behind in school, some so significantly that they qualified for special education by the third or fourth grade. When given strategies to draw and write about their thinking, their reading improved significantly. Some of the visual motor learners I have worked with used drawing and writing to bring themselves up to grade level in reading and writing. We have a whole class of learners who are not getting their needs met at school because they are not being given what they need to succeed. With these students, typically they are given more of the instruction that doesn't work for them in a slowed down fashion. This does not result in learning for them, but rather they fall further and further behind. So, instead of phonics or other instruction based on sounds and letters, these students need to draw and write to learn to read.

Drawing provides the motor movement necessary to create mental images for the visual motor learner (Arwood, 2011). This works because of the evolutionary connection between the hand, eye, and language within the brain (Wilson, 1998). When we create a shape with our hand, the same shape is represented mentally in the visual system. Many teachers believe that in order to learn to read students must learn the letter sound correspondences and learn to read with sound. However, while this works great for some students, there are others for whom working with sounds and letters never results in reading. For these students their access to reading is through drawing and writing. Both drawing and writing provide visual motor input so that visual motor learners can access their thinking in the way that they learn. The process of acquiring concepts to think and language to express those concepts is turned on its head for visual motor learners. These learners need to draw the ideas so they can see what is happening and who is doing what (this provides context). Then they need to label the ideas on the drawing and use the labels as the foundation for writing about what they drew. Finally, they can read back what they wrote (Arwood, 2011). Instead of the usual read, write, maybe draw, that we typically see in schools, these learners need to draw, write, and then read. Think about it. If you draw, you can see what your ideas are. By labeling the drawing, the conventional written language is added. By writing, the learner acquires the conventional shapes of written ideas which then can be read back. In other words, if you can write it from memory, you can automatically read the idea. The reverse is not necessarily true.

We can also ask students to draw ideas that they read to find out if they understood the text. This allows the teacher to see the learner's thinking and therefore, be able to help the student to understand the text if the drawing does not match the written ideas (Arwood, 2011). When a teacher sees that the learner's drawing does not match the text, the ideas that are missing are the ideas within the text that the student did not understand. The teacher can then guide the learners to look up the ideas (words) that were not understood and refine their drawing to match the text. These and other drawing and writing strategies can be found within Arwood's Viconic Language Methods™ based on her Neurosemantic Language Learning Theory (Arwood, 2011). This revolutionary learning theory is based on Arwood's triangulation of literature from neuroscience, cognitive psychology, and language and explains that most learners today are visual learners and therefore, need visual thinking strategies that match their visual thinking.

There are many possible activities we can offer to learners to help them acquire new concepts and language. One of these is Story Pictures. Story Pictures are pictures of people doing things together that we can view together with learners and tell stories, draw stories, write stories, and read back the stories. Using open ended Story Pictures allows learners to acquire both the concepts found within the Story Pictures and also the language necessary to express those concepts. When working with learners using Story Pictures, we can help them acquire language and greater cognition by using the eight processes of literacy. An example of a Story Picture is INSL LLC Story Picture # 6, Give It To Me!.

Story Picture # 6 Give It To Me!

The first literacy processes we use when starting to work with a Story Picture are viewing and speaking. Learners can view the Story Picture and then tell the story they see in the picture. As other learners hear the story, they are engaging in the process of listening. Learners can take turns speaking and listening. Next, learners can draw the ideas they see in the picture. The process of drawing also involves using the process of calculating. In order to draw what we see, we must mentally calculate the spatial locations and relative size of people and objects we wish to draw. Once the learner has made a drawing of the Story Picture, the teacher can listen to the learner tell their story about the picture and write the ideas in the form of labels directly onto the learner's drawing. The learner can then use the labels to create a visual dictionary of the ideas labeled on the drawing. A visual dictionary shows the written idea adjacent to a drawn idea that shows the meaning of the written idea. This way, learners can both develop conventional spelling as well as learn the meanings of the written ideas. Next, the learner can write a story about the picture using both the teacher's labels and the visual dictionary to help in the writing process. Finally, the learner completes the cycle of eight literacy processes by reading the story they wrote.

In the following student examples, a five-year-old worked together with the mother and the teacher to draw and write a story about INSL LLC **Story Picture # 6 Give It To Me!** The learner told the story seen in the picture and then drew those ideas and wrote about the ideas. The question was asked, "I wonder what is going to happen next?" and the learner made up a story of what might happen next and did all the drawing as the mother worked to write the labels onto the drawing hand-over-hand together. The child drew and wrote the ideas onto a visual dictionary. Next, the child told the mother the story the child wanted to write, and they wrote it together hand-over-hand. Finally, the learner read back what was written.

Example of a comic strip and visual dictionary made by a five-year-old

ED. Matadores

By adding the eighth process of literacy to our instruction, we are honoring all children and providing a way for visual and visual-motor learners to acquire language and literacy.

Free Offer

Do you have questions about drawing as the eighth literacy? Connect with Dr. Lou for a free connection call. Are you ready to learn more and try a great new learning product? Use this special offer to get 10% off on the Story Pictures plus Manual bundle.

Maryjane Sander M.Ed
https://institutensl.com

Maryjane Sander has been teaching in a self-contained special education classroom for over 17 years. She has three sons, the youngest of whom has autism and a cognitive delay. Maryjane received her Master's Degree in Education at the University of Portland with a focus on Neuroeducation, where her capstone project was on using the Viconic language methods (Neuro methods that are used in the InstituteNSL clinic) in her classroom and showing the growth in her students over a four-year time span. Currently, she is using Viconic Language methods exclusively in her instruction. She has been involved with using these methods professionally for four years and uses them personally with her own son who has autism. Maryjane continues to find great success with the methods used in the clinic both in her personal and professional life.

Using A Visual Teaching Method
By Maryjane Sander, M.ED.

I am a special education teacher at a public school in southwest Washington State. It is one of the largest public school districts in southwest Washington with five high schools. As a special education teacher, I figured out within the first two years of my career that teaching differently-abled students to read using traditional techniques just did not work. Then, I began a quest to find a method that did work for my students. I discovered Neuro Education through the University of Portland, and using brain-based instruction has completely changed my teaching methods.

Specifically, according to Cooper (2006), literacy is defined as reading, writing, speaking, listening, viewing, thinking, and calculating. I would argue that there is a missing aspect to literacy, and drawing is missing from the list (Debreczeny, 2023)

History of teaching

According to Edgar (2012), the United States educational system currently assumes that the most effective way to teach literacy is by breaking down the information to be taught into tiny pieces and asking students to reassemble those pieces back together in their brains. A great deal of how we think about teaching was influenced by behaviorism, which was introduced by B.F Skinner (1953). Skinner introduced the idea that when given a certain stimulus, an outside force could control and predict an action or reaction in a person, such as, if the teacher said "beach" all students would draw the exact same beach, or, if the teacher said "3x5" all students would know that is 15 if they had been told. This led to the idea that if all teachers gave the same stimulus to their students in the same way, then all students would provide the same output back to the educator. In turn, this would provide evidence that all students had learned. By using this approach all teachers could teach from the same plans, and all students could theoretically be successful. The widespread adoption of practices stemming from behaviorism led to curriculum designers breaking down the parts of literacy into smaller pieces; this is referred to as task analysis. According to Edgar (2012), current teaching practices continue to use Behaviorism and task analysis as a sizable portion of the curriculum. New teachers are being trained to embrace these older ideals, and although there is evidence that increasing numbers of students are struggling using these methods, teachers are nevertheless encouraged to try more of the same. The result of using this method is that for the past 50 years, we have continued to attempt to teach all children the same way, using drills, testing facts, and expecting students to memorize what they are learning. Then, we test students by having them regurgitate what they have just "learned" (Arwood, Rostamizadeh, 2018).

A new idea

One theory, the Neurosemantic Language Learning Theory (NsLLT), was developed over many years by Arwood (1983, 2011). This theory describes how humans learn through the neurobiological process associated with the processing of sensory input and human language. The NsLLT has expanded to include many learning strategies and educational practices that are referred to as Viconic Language Methods™ (Arwood 2011). These methods promote language acquisition in children by providing them with semantic information in ways that their brains can process, which uses their strengths to allow them to gain academic information.

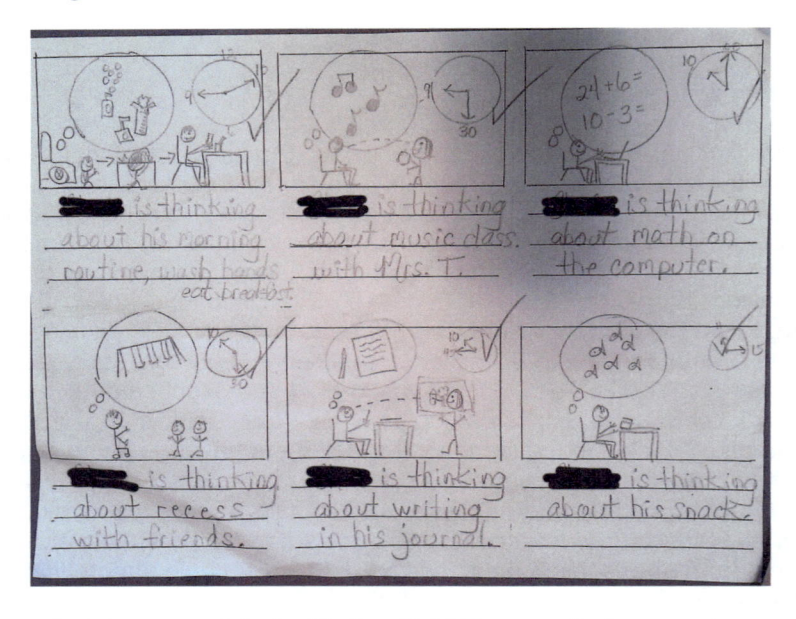

The principles associated with the NsLLT argue that concepts are not taught to children; instead, all concepts must be acquired by children over time through the assignment of meaning by adults and peers. According to this theory, there are two diverse ways that humans learn, which are based upon the neurobiological composition of their brains from birth. This means that some children are auditory thinkers while others are visual thinkers. Auditory concepts are made with the overlap of sound and sight (Arwood, 2011). When an auditory learner has created enough of these patterns, he can create new concepts with just the sound of another person's voice or even with the sound of his own voice. The current population of students is made up of people of whom only 10-15% are auditory thinkers. (Arwood, 2011). On the other hand, visual thinkers are people who need to see concepts to create ideas in their brains. According to Arwood (2011), even though 85-90% of our population are visual thinkers, most educators still predominantly use auditory methods of instruction (such as phonics, memorizing, and repeating things such as times tables, lecturing to students, and spelling lists).

Rather than using these traditional auditory methods of teaching, visual learners need visual thinking strategies which include adding the eighth process of literacy, drawing. A particularly good way to introduce students to drawing and writing about concepts and ideas is to use the story pictures that are produced by The Institute for Neurosemantic and Sociocognitive Learning (https://institutensl.com). These pictures provide a representation of a story that could be true and very open-ended. There are multiple people interacting with each other, which teaches students about relationships between people and helps them to think about other people and what they might be thinking. Showing these pictures to students and talking about the relationships between the people and what they are doing together and what they might be thinking opens up a world of ideas for writing. I often "tag" the picture with a word that the students might need in their writing. This same picture is used for an entire week of writing and reading instruction which makes planning easy. They ensure that students learn in the method, which is beneficial to their brains, which is to draw, write, then read, rather than read, write, then draw. Students who are visual learners (about 85+% of our learners) often will learn to write before they learn to read so I use these pictures to elicit writing in even my youngest learners. Students do their own learning by drawing and writing about most everything that they are learning about. This allows students to create their own meaning about what is going on around them.

Using a visual method of teaching

Visual methods of instruction are designed to help students acquire functional language and concepts rather than simply providing the patterns of information that are currently being taught today. It is important to help students acquire concepts (actual ideas) rather than patterns which are just memorized items such as letters and letter sounds, times tables, and memorizing facts because the concepts will stay permanently in the brain, and other concepts and ideas can be learned by attaching different concepts together (Arwood 2011).

To create concepts and language, the learner must be able to create meaning from the drawing. This means that they can attach their own language to the drawing and add their own ideas and concepts to build on what the educator has drawn. When educators draw in real-time, they are also adding acoustic patterns by talking about the pictures to the visual patterns that they are creating. Adding these patterns together helps to create meaning for those students who can incorporate auditory input with visual input (Arwood 2011).

STORY PICTURES

Understand, Implement, and Adapt the Use of Story Pictures to Help Your Learner Comprehend Complex Ideas.

DRAW   WRITE   READ

The other aspect of drawing together with students is that educators create a social interaction with students, which in and of itself helps create functional language, especially for those students who cannot make meaning from listening alone (Newman & Latifi, 2021, Vygotsky, 1962). These drawings are always done in real-time to allow for multi-sensory input into the brain. As the student watches the hand move across the paper, their eyes act as sensory receptors to take in the lines and react to the edges of the objects by creating a concept in their own mind. The learner must be able to create meaning from these pictures, and as the educator is drawing, they are adding language to the drawing. This creates a shared symbol between the educator and the student which gives the student some agency in the process (meaning they are a part of the process). When the student and the educator have a shared symbol, they have something that they can talk, draw, write, and read about (Arwood, 2011).

Another technique associated with visual language acquisition involves requiring students to use their own drawings to conceptualize their thinking. The first two stages of learning (sensory input and creating patterns) work the same for this as they do for the drawing for your students. When students are visual thinkers, translating their thoughts right into words can be as difficult as translating information from one language to another (Arwood, Robb, & Rostamizadeh 2018). If the students can take the step of taking their ideas, which are visual, and translating those to a picture that they have drawn, they create a shared referent (which is a common frame of reference) with the teacher, which can then help them turn their visual ideas into writing. After the teacher and the student look over their shared referent, they can discuss what will be in the writing, and then the teacher can help the student by labeling the picture. The student can then take those labels and write. This helps to reduce the stress on the brain of spelling or sounding out words (Arwood, Robb, & Rostamizadeh 2018).

By visually labeling a drawing with the teacher, the students can just draw the shapes of the words rather than trying to use their auditory system of sounding or spelling these words out. This way the students are not tied down by auditory methods such as not knowing the spelling of words. By drawing their ideas instead of being asked to orally explain them, the students can then translate their drawings into writing on their paper. Especially if the students have a visual learning system, this helps them to take the acoustic patterns out of their writing and just focus on their strengths, which are visual patterns, such as seeing the shape of the word rather than "sounding it out" and drawing their writing before putting words to it.

All these methods incorporate drawing into the learning. To gain concepts, students need layers of information that overlap to make a change in the brain. Studies show that children can show more of their thinking with drawing than they can articulate in words (Hong, Broderick, & McAuliffe, 2021). This is especially true for students who have visual thinking. Due to the visual system being the one that is most meaningful for most students (Arwood, 2011), using visual movement-based instruction like drawing becomes essential for creating those layers in the brain which eventually become concepts and language around those concepts. The research presented here overwhelmingly suggests that drawing, for most students, is the most efficient way for them to learn, write, read, acquire language, and become literate.

SOCIAL EMOTIONAL LEARNING & DIVERSITY, EQUITY, AND INCLUSION

Sam Aquino Drohin
Founder

I am a parent of four children, and have observed the academic experiences of my children and others in the k-12 system and beyond. I have come to believe that the current education system is not preparing students for the challenges of the 21st century. The goal is to change the future for children and adults across the globe by addressing four key challenges: readiness for the next step, affordability, accessibility, and relevance. Education should prepare students to be what the world needs today and tomorrow, not who was needed over 100 years ago. I am committed to creating an education system that empowers all learners to reach their full potential and become contributing members of society.

Bridging The Gap: Modernizing Education For Today And Tomorrow
By Sam Aquino Drohin

In the ever-evolving landscape of education, one visionary academic stands at the forefront, armed with innovative ideas and a steadfast commitment to Bridging the Gap between traditional learning methods and the demands of the modern world.

Introduction and Context: A Passion for Modernizing Education

Academia Modo Profesional was founded with the primary goal of exploring and implementing modern training and education techniques to change the way we view how we learn in the K–12 system through colleges and universities, all the way through professional development and continuing education. I am the founder and CEO of Academia Modo Profesional and have been working to get our project management course live. My experience as a trainer has been primarily in the sales and project management spaces, where I've developed methods and a deeper understanding of empathy, persuasion, problem-solving, and conflict resolution. In the education space, I have worked with educators to review the curriculum to be developed, worked at the state level supporting the public school systems throughout the state of Wisconsin, and tutored other students to help them achieve their academic goals. My advocacy work has ranged from individual student advocacy to speaking in front of the state Joint Finance Committee about funding for the Wisconsin Technical College System to DEI work in academic and professional environments. These experiences have provided the foundation for this effort to modernize education.

The missions of Ed Matadores and Academia Modo Profesional are closely aligned and demonstrate that more than one organization sees the need for change in our education systems. Effective change requires many people to be aligned to the same goals, and when working together, their chances to succeed increase. Ed Matadores is operating as this unifying force to help drive this change.

Problem - Solution Identification: Overcoming Resistance to Change Innovation

We're beginning with some of the same things as other organizations by leveraging Project Based and Social Emotional Learning.
(Photo by Marija Zaric on Unsplash)

Where we differ is that we are starting at what could be considered the end of the education journey by focusing on training and continuous education for those already in the workforce with plans to work our way backward by reimagining college and, ultimately, the K-12 system.

In general, education and training currently leverage a one-size-fits-all approach. Instances of individualized learning plans are becoming more common. Still, the foundation of those plans is often based on a requirement to complete a specific course that has been predefined based on what all students should do. A key objective of the modernized structure is to ensure students are ready for the next level in their academic or professional journey by tying concepts to the next steps while ensuring the curriculum is relevant to their journey.

Children often have challenges with wanting to complete coursework when they do not understand how it ties into something they will encounter down the road; a common question when they are taking algebra is, "When will I ever use this in life?" and the answers to that question are often lacking the direction they need to help them understand the importance of learning the material. Adult continuing education is often used to continue membership or licensing, and in many cases, does not foster learning through hands-on experiences; in short, it's often a matter of listening to a lecture or talk and may have a small quiz at the end to say you completed the coursework while still failing to deliver on the premise of substantive skill development. College and university courses tend to fall somewhere in the middle of those gaps highlighted for K-12 education and professional development courses. The adjustments to our education will do two things:

1. Ensure students have what they need before moving from their current curriculum to the next level, whether a new grade, a new job, or a higher-level position within the same job class.
2. Students will have the confidence needed to get from where they are today to where they need to be tomorrow without guessing so much.

The Approach

The guiding principle behind our approach is based on tested approaches in tutoring, classroom, and training environments. The philosophy is simple: keep the student and their needs in mind, and the approach can follow from there. Some students are ready to jump in and try while others may need encouragement and extra examples before feeling confident. One key observation with students in all environments is their engagement level being maintained or increased when the content is relevant, relatable, and understood.

Expected Results

The primary outcome of this work is to ensure students are ready for what comes ahead. If they are taking a professional development course, they can begin applying what was learned on day one if the student is taking a course at the K-12 or post-secondary level; then they understand how the material ties into what comes next, and those skills learned come with an understanding of how they can be applied to the real world.

- Education tends to stick better with students when they understand what they're doing, where they are going, and when they have the confidence to execute what they've learned. By emphasizing a focus on their educational experiences and outcomes beyond simply passing a test or getting a good grade, we can have long-lasting positive impacts.
- Students will benefit from being able to tie ideas to other areas of their personal and professional lives; educators and trainers will have more relevant conversations with their students about how the concepts being taught may be used and get beyond simply teaching the material.

(Photo by Slidebean on Unsplash)

Challenges

There are several challenges to achieving a modern education model. Educators may need training to implement new methodologies and tools, which can become expensive and time-consuming in an environment where funding and limited time are constant challenges. Changes to existing curricula and integrating new methods into existing curricula can take a lot of time as well. Standardized testing and mandated curriculum present a challenge where the material being taught may be to pass a course or test rather than ensuring the proper outcomes for students. The Evaluation and Assessment of new methods can be complex and may not appropriately or sufficiently capture the benefits or outcomes of modern and innovative approaches.

Educational policies and regulations can also create barriers to achieving new educational models. Traditional metrics might not be enough to determine if modern approaches are effective.

(Photo by Towfiqu Barbhuiya on Unsplash)

Resistance to change, resource limitations, and technological barriers are some elements we need to contend with. Policymakers, educators, administrators, and parents may be used to the traditional education system and have difficulty conceptualizing and adjusting to new approaches that sound, look, and feel different from what they have become familiar with. Educators are a crucial part of the success of any new academic approach, and they will need to be convinced of the benefits and what successful execution looks like to ensure adoption and advancement in this space. Many parents, administrators, and policymakers may have a very specific set of expectations around what education should look like based on their own experiences; deviating from these expectations may cause resistance. Cultures and communities can also have different views on education, furthering the need to adopt a model that does not rely on a one-size-fits-all approach.

The resources available for schools are primarily based on the affluence or wealth of those communities. Lower-income communities will have a higher challenge in meeting a specific school's need for investments in technology, training, curriculum development, and other needed resources to be successful. The concern around resource availability becomes compounded by disparities at the student or family level with access to technology differing from home to home; this creates disparities in learning opportunities when implementing technology-based solutions.

These challenges often give would-be innovators and change champions a sense of defeat before starting. In a space where stakeholder skepticism can cause pushback and resource challenges can be difficult to overcome, there are things we can begin doing now to address these concerns. Many schools in the K-12 system, public and private, are exploring alternatives and sharing what they've learned along the way. The training and professional development industry has a wide array of approaches and platforms that can also give hints of success.

By beginning, not just with the end in mind, but at the end with training and professional development, we can work on the elements needed to get students the skills they need to perform in their jobs. This also gives us insights into the gaps and enables us to look back at universities and colleges to identify opportunities for improvement and modernization around job readiness.

Community is another component that needs to be addressed.
Education does not begin or end in the classroom; it starts and ends at home and the community. Any efforts to modernize education need to be met with the education of parents and communities to expedite adoption and increase our potential for success.

Your Story: Reimagining our Education Model

The journey to achieve a new education model started with developing a professional training course. While supporting another organization as a trainer, I began to see glimpses of the changes needed and began to partner with school faculty and staff across the nation. Through various work sessions, we began to identify an approach for social-emotional and project-based learning models. The approach for the professional development course has been beta-tested and is now being finalized. The next step after deploying this course is to develop a professional development course analogous to a degree-bearing program to achieve completion within a year. From there, we plan on working through the K-12 system to transform learning and outcomes. One question I hope to answer is, "Do we really need to use the current 12-year structure?"

Your Call for Revolution

Modernizing education isn't limited to classrooms; it ripples into homes and communities. By engaging parents, neighbors, and mentors, we create a collective force driving positive change in education. By working with our systems, educators, trainers, and communities, we can go beyond simply learning facts and help establish the "why" to help students have confidence in applying the knowledge acquired and understand the steps they will take once they finish their coursework.

Contact Me: https://linktr.ee/sam.aquino

ED. Matadores

Dr. Joe Griffin
President and CEO of Joe Griffin Global Consulting LLC

Dr. Joe Griffin is an educational consultant, motivational speaker, professor, and author with success as a teacher and administrator on all levels of education, including K-12, junior college, and university experience. Dr. Griffin hails from "The Home Of The Blues", Clarksdale, Mississippi, and his record of turning around schools, including moving one of his high schools from a D to a B for the first time in school history, precedes him. Dr. Griffin was able to overcome the influences of gang wars and racial tension in his community, despite being raised by a single parent, to accomplish his dream of playing college basketball on academic and athletic scholarships, jumpstarting his educational journey.

Dr. Griffin used his passion and diversity to attain a range of degrees that began with an A.A. and a B.A. in English from HBCU Coahoma Community College in Clarksdale, MS and from private Belhaven University in Jackson, MS. He later gained 24 graduate hours in English from the University of West Alabama after attaining a master's degree in secondary education from Delta State University. His specialist degree and doctoral studies in Educational Leadership and Research were completed at the University of Southern Mississippi, Hattiesburg, MS.

Dr. Griffin's initial research, *Discipline-culture and Instructional Practices: An Integrated Leader's Role (2020)* has expanded into the Three Pillar DIPP Approach Framework, comprising the *DIPP Approach for Educators Success Manual,* the *DIPP Approach for Student and Adult Success: An SEL Curriculum for Life* and accompanying *DIPP Approach for Student and Adult Success Guidebook,* and the Integration of the Arts as Therapy Pillar with his three book *Spirit, Heart, and Soul* poetry collection. Ultimately, Griffin believes, "All people can have success, no matter where one comes from... And they all deserve that chance."

DIPP Approach Framework for Future Success
By Dr. Joe Griffin

Humble Beginnings

Reared by a single mother in one of the nation's poorest regions, the Mississippi Delta, in the "Home of the Blues," Clarksdale, Mississippi, I had to do something to inspire change in education. I did not know that I would become the CEO of Joe Griffin Global Consulting LLC, where our mission is to empower and equip educators through SEL-based (socioemotional learning) strategies that influence discipline culture, instructional practices, and performance for all (DIPP). Our award-winning, three-tier model, DIPP Approach Framework, puts both students and adults in a position to be successful in schools and in life.

I've been fortunate enough to teach and be an administrator on every level of K-12 education and to teach at the community college and university levels. Additionally, I've helped raise student achievement at five schools as principal, have served in various capacities in diverse rural and urban settings with predominantly black, white, and Latino, and worked at a French Immersion school... and I've relied on this approach to improve performance for all in each situation. The DIPP Approach Framework has been applied and implemented in both mega and small schools. The practitioner strategies used in the DIPP Approach Framework originate from my dissertation research, where I coined the term discipline-culture, the way teachers and administrators handle issues daily within schools and how this affects the instructional practices that they are willing to use. Moreover, the consideration of educators' feelings as well as students' feelings has long been a topic of discussion within my research and practice.

Using the DIPP Approach Framework

The DIPP Approach Framework for educational revolution is deeply rooted in SEL, relying heavily on the tenets of self-awareness, self-management, social awareness, relationship-building, and making responsible decisions to accelerate personal development (*DIPP Approach for Student and Adult Success: An SEL Curriculum for Life* along with the *DIPP Approach for Student and Adult Success Guidebook*). Other anchors for the framework are the Educational Leadership Success Pillar (e-book, *Igniting the Spark: DIPP Approach to Educational Revolution* and *the DIPP Approach for Educators Success Manual*) and the Integration of the Arts as Therapy Pillar (*Spirit, Heart, and Soul Poetry Collection-* 3 books). Furthermore, integrated leadership, Marks and Printy (2003), the combination of instructional and transformational leadership practices, is the foundational strategy that allows educators to use both motivational and instructional techniques to influence schools to move forward.

Dr. Joe's DIPP Approach Framework
A THREE-PILLAR MODEL SCHOOL AND LIFE TRANSFORMATION

EDUCATIONAL LEADERSHIP SUCCESS PILLAR		SOCIOEMOTIONAL LEARNING (SEL) AND PERSONAL DEVELOPMENT PILLAR		INTEGRATION OF THE ARTS AS THERAPY PILLAR (SPIRIT, HEART, AND SOUL COLLECTION)	
Igniting the Spark	QR		QR	Home Blues	QR
DIPP Approach	QR	DIPP Guidebook	QR		QR
		Spirit, Heart, and Soul Collection of Poetry		Dream Season	QR

As a member of various teams since my elementary years, I have always been aware of the multiple roles and responsibilities on a team because I have gone from bench warmer to starter and vice versa. Still, the idea is to always keep the goal of the team in mind. Our goal is to win! We win when we move any academic needle, no matter how minimal or maximum it is considered to be. Celebrating wins and milestones is important because it guides the work to be done and measures commitment. After going through high school and college as a high-performing student-athlete, and after serving as a substitute teacher, bus driver, teacher, lead teacher, and assistant principal, it was easy for me to navigate schools as a principal because of my understanding of roles and relationships, which would become the crust of my evolution as a leader. As a team captain, which is ultimately what principalship is, leaders should ensure that teammates are joyful, well, cooperative, and engaged in the work. Steering the ship as a leader while using DIPP approach strategies and philosophy led to many successes, and it is through this lens that I share all accomplishments with teammates because I work with and through people continuously.

Missions May Merge

The Ed Matadores mission of revolutionizing the educational system provides synergy with the DIPP Approach. Undoubtedly, we have to do something different unless we want to keep getting the same results within the educational landscape. Rethinking how we operate in and around schools is crucial in connecting with new-age students, adults, and forward-thinkers. Change is inevitable, and frankly, our educational systems are broken across the land, making the revolution even more important, necessary, and immediate.

The DIPP Approach Framework is a system of methods that has proven to immediately improve school environments when implemented with fidelity and consistency. Planning is essential when creating a SELF-motivated school to ensure that students and adults flourish daily. Actions must be intentional and purposeful to garner positive outcomes. The DIPP Approach Framework solves the challenge of adapting leadership to ensure students and adults are joyful and well while reaching academic excellence.

My Passion For the DIPP Approach Framework

As a highly emotional young man, I realized early on about attachment and detachment from individuals based on how I was made to feel. I noticed that I did not treat them well in return because of this, and I determined that I would always make sure people knew how much I cared for them. I noticed this same coordination of feelings within locker rooms as an athlete and later as a coach, within English classrooms as a teacher, then later as a professor, as a lead teacher, and then later as a turnaround change agent. It wasn't until then that I realized an entire framework for implementing school reform was in the making. I am determined to lead in a different way, no matter the venue or area of leadership. Furthermore, the DIPP Approach allows space for creativity, originality, and individuality in a collaborative environment that focuses on empowering all stakeholders. As individuals get better and stronger, so does the team as a collective unit.

For too long, especially in educational spaces, we have ignored the well-being of students and adults, treating school like something from a horror book by terrifying some and torturing others. We can fix these problems with the DIPP Approach Framework, especially when all tiers of the model are used simultaneously to create harmony, student prowess, and relentlessness to increase performance for all.

Leaders and Success

It's important to note that before having success as a school leader, I failed as a school leader. Before learning to transfer my team-oriented attitude to professional service, I had a quick but large learning curve. I did not see a correlation of being on a team in athletics to that of being on a team as an administrator. Learning that it was not just up to stakeholders to buy into change, but that it was also up to leaders to inspire change created the biggest shift in my mentality toward leadership. It's true that everything starts with leadership, but everything does not end with leadership. Vision requires help and support when the vision is worthy.

Early on in my leadership journey, I tried to do nearly everything on my own, without the assistance of teammates, before I learned the importance of distributive leadership principles and before I learned more extensively about relationships in the workplace. Empowerment principles are deeply rooted within the walls of the DIPP Approach Framework. Experience is often the best teacher as it teaches us the good and bad of what we encounter.

As a young teacher and coach, I was able to push the young men on the basketball team to a championship, but as an administrator, I was also dependent on individuals to ensure transformation and productivity were transferred to others. That was not an easy connection for me to make initially, but I eventually learned to master on-the-job buy-in by creating relationships. Once I learned the importance of relationships, the instructional practices and performance pieces fell in place, and I have expounded my compilations into the DIPP Approach Framework. SEL for all lives here!

Parent and Community Engagement

Parent and community engagement are crucial within the DIPP Approach Framework. Multiple meeting opportunities are given to parents each month, and community relations are at a premium. Information is easily accessible, and out-of-the-box events such as Family Reunion Style Open Houses for parent-teacher meetings, Career Expositions to give students access to professionals, and Learning Walks for different groups are in rotation. School-wide and departmental initiatives also spread throughout the building.

DIPP Approach Proven Results

The embedded principles of the DIPP Approach for Educators were formed during my 23-plus years in public education. The strategies used within the DIPP Approach Framework are planned, purposeful, and continual works-in-progress. There is no time limit or length for implementation. All strategies within the *DIPP Approach for Educators Success Manual* are SEL-embedded practices that make teamwork necessary for success and survival. I used these strategies to turn around five schools in the following predicaments:
1. Moved a Top 15 worst school in the state to a successful rating within three years.
2. Moved 20+ percentage points in over three subjects in the same year.
3. Prepared a school for state takeover, still moving up in every area the same year.
4. Led a school out-of-state takeover, increasing percentage points during the process.
5. Led a school from a D to a B in one year, for the first time in the history of the school, maintaining the status for four years thereafter.

Challenges to Change

Whenever there is a call-to-action or whenever new approaches or initiatives are established, you will face some obstacles during implementation. Just as no leader has ever dodged scrutiny, neither has a program, even when the intent is to improve the well-being of those on the frontlines. Challenge to change is to be expected, and when you are committed to the process, you will overcome the obstacles associated with implementation. More than 90% of the time, it is a mindset issue that hinders progress. When you are able to reprogram the mind, you have a chance with that individual. The DIPP Approach calls for us to truly care for one another's well-being, creating a trusting environment for influence. Mindsets around education and leadership have to change in order to rethink discipline in schools because discipline-culture plus instructional practices equals performance (DIPP). Discipline occurs not only with students but also with adults, and it makes sense to think that these interactions affect performance. The discussion is about what educators are willing to do because there is no doubt that they can! Ultimately, the DIPP Approach Framework proves to be invaluable to not only students but educators alike. Let's DIPP into the future!

Free Offer
Building an SEL-motivated environment is not easy to do, but Dr. Griffin has mastered the concept of creating collaborative educational spaces where students and adults thrive. Therefore, readers and leaders who wish to immerse themselves further into the DIPP mindset through a FREE discovery call with Dr. Joe Griffin, or to learn more about the DIPP Approach Framework for Future Success, should feel free to contact him by email at joe@drjoegriffinspeaks.com or by phone at 662 313-6018.

Website: www.drjoegriffinspeaks.com

Contact Joe Griffin

https://www.linkedin.com/in/joegriffinphd

https://drive.google.com/file/d/1cXzcUnDmnlf7vRp1KygFXfkKFWuiVh5U/view?usp=drive_link

Cindy Starke M.D, Ph.D.

Dr. Cindy Starke is a board-certified internal medicine physician with a Ph.D. in Molecular Genetics. She teaches audiences to use the power of their subconscious minds to challenge their preconceived notions of what they are capable of to unleash the champion inside. The award-winning author of "From Fear and Failure to the Finish Line- Unleash Your Potential and Discover the Champion Within", she shows you how to embrace the most powerful version of yourself!

Empowering Educators: Nurturing the Seeds of Personal Growth by Unveiling Blind Spots in Your Subconscious Mind
By Dr. Cindy Starke

Imagine a classroom where the teacher walks in with a sense of purpose, inner peace, and a commitment to personal growth. Such teachers not only impart knowledge but also inspire, uplift, and guide the future. As we embark on this journey into the heart of education, let us remember the words of Albert Einstein, who said, 'The value of education is not the learning of many facts, but the training of the mind to think.' In this chapter, we delve into the vital need for teachers to thrive personally, for it is in their flourishing that the seeds of a brighter future are sown.

Escaping Sexual Abuse with the Power of Higher Education

I am Cindy Starke, a physician, geneticist, mother, and dream doctor. I have been fascinated with human 'potentiality' since I was 15 years old. Beneath this remarkable pursuit lies a story of resilience forged in the face of adversity.

I grew up in a blue-collar family where my dad was an electrician, and my mother was a hairdresser. My brother and my sister were much older than I was, and after high school, they both immediately began vocational work, similar to my parents. My life's narrative is a testament to the transformative power of my experiences and motivation to explore the subconscious. This leads me to motivate teachers to shift their narrative and nurture the seeds of personal "growth".

In my early days, I navigated a completely different path. I was not in alignment with either one of my parent's lines of work. Through an unfortunate exposure to alcohol and drugs, teenagers living with us who had gotten kicked out of their houses, and a series of incidents of being sexually violated by my brother's friends, I had a strong desire to get myself free from what my childhood hometown represented. It is from this place of adversity and self-discovery that I embarked on a remarkable journey; eventually, I realized that to nurture others, I had to first nurture myself. I left home and became not only the first person in my family to go to college, I got a bachelor's degree in genetics, graduating magna cum laude, but I also obtained both an MD and a Ph.D. at Emory University on a full-ride scholarship.

I loved academics. The university, in both undergraduate and graduate settings, allowed me to challenge myself and be seen as crucial to what I could contribute in a scholarly way, in a gender-non-specific way. My sexuality didn't matter. Drugs and alcohol were no longer present, women were no longer sexually used and abused, and men and women were seen as equals. I continued my fascination with questioning typical societal boundaries and expectations.

Hospital Medicine to Ironman Triathlon

After practicing medicine for two decades, caring for over 100,000 patients, and becoming a mother to two amazing children, I pushed my human limits again at age 47, taught myself how to bike and swim long distances, and completed an Ironman Triathlon in Naples, Florida. This remarkable athletic feat opened my eyes to what is possible in a human's body as I have always seen myself as not having an ounce of athleticism. I also began an unquenchable desire to help people become truly healthy in their lives, not only with their physical health, which is what I had been attempting to accomplish at the bedsides of America, but also with their minds. I wanted to help people "master the matter between their ears." I believe that a person's narrowly skewed beliefs of the societal constructs of success they were allowed to have in the world held people back in ways they should never have

I started reading every book I could on the subconscious mind. I became a master practitioner in neurolinguistic programming, and I got certified in a trauma release method technique to help rid people of the negative effects of people, places, and things that they encountered either in their childhood or into adulthood that were unintentionally holding them back.

Helping Others Find the Way

In 2018, I became the visionary, CEO, and founder of an online program called "Soul Circle Academy", where men and women in the second halves of their lives come together and learn how the subconscious mind works and how truly powerful it is. We specifically work with the reticular activating system. This is the part of the subconscious mind that is the filtering system for all our beliefs. We work together to clear out everything present that is holding them back from impact and greatness in health, work, relationships, self-worth, confidence, and life.

I have seen great results in my group coaching programs with doctors, lawyers, nurses, teachers, and everyone else under the sun. Mothers and fathers have been successfully breaking out of generational limitations and cycles of abuse. By clearing the influences, emotions, and beliefs from the reticular activating system, you can have full access to 100% of the potentiality of your brain. Otherwise, if the subconscious mind is riddled with societal, educational, religious, and parental programming, you are literally only able to see the opportunities that are in your life based on what was shown to you in your childhood. Once the programming is cleared, the subconscious mind can relay to my clients accurately all that is available to them in the world. My clients have overcome burnout, stood up for themselves in the workplace, set boundaries with their loved ones, and have had ongoing success in having deep, emotionally satisfying relationships with their kids, spouses, coworkers, and members of their communities.

Semantics of the Subconscious Mind

Most people think that we can see everything in our conscious minds in front of us. But what actually happens is that everything we encounter in life bypasses our brain's frontal lobe, and is then filtered through the reticular activating system. Any information that does not line up with our societal, religious, and family programming gets deleted, distorted, or generalized and is then presented back to our frontal cortex and processed as reality. We are literally living figments of our imagination. We can only see and experience the opportunities around us that are in congruence with everything that we have seen and lived and witnessed, and experienced in our lifetimes up to this present moment.

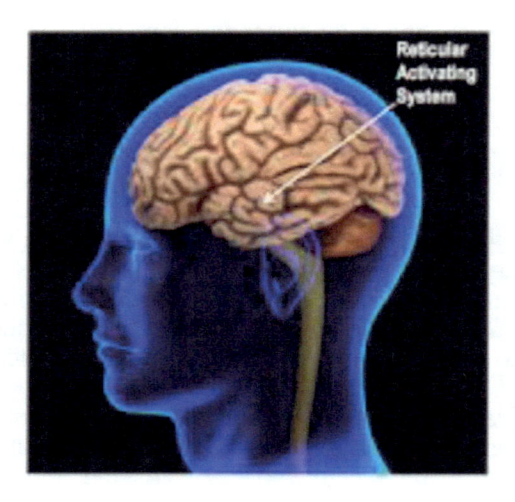

Your programming is almost entirely in place by age 7. The way our conscious and subconscious mind interacts and communicates with each other makes it physically and genetically impossible for you to comprehend all that is available to you when all your filtering system is clogged up with generations and generations of negativity and trauma and small-mindedness.

Today, we bring this transformative journey to the forefront of education, shining a light on the need for teachers to take action and redefine how they impart knowledge. Teachers have the crucial task of speaking greatness to all their students morning, noon, and night for years on end. In the early 1960s, three psychologists, Wolfgang Kohler, Max Wertheimer, and Kurt Koffka, termed the parts of our subconscious mind that house the emotions as gestalt. When the gestalt for sadness is completely filled, and at its limit, it shows up as depression. The gestalt for anger overflowing results in rage, fear overflowing results in anxiety, and guilt overwhelming results in shame.

Vibrational Scale of Consciousness

There is a vibrational scale of consciousness created by David Hawkins, Ph.D., that I refer to and use as a model for personal growth. The lower the frequency of emotions, such as sadness, fear, and grief, the more energy is constricted in the body. Higher frequencies, such as grace and joy, conversely represent an expanded state of consciousness, close to the transcendence of the soul, closer to our Creator as you see that entity. Shame as an emotion vibrates at a frequency of 20 Hz, whereas death starts to vibrate at a score of 25 Hz. So unregulated, we are quite literally "shaming ourselves to death". However, when we can regulate our gestalts by dealing with those events that have filled them up since we were born, we can resource ourselves at the moment. We can be more effective mothers and fathers, teachers and coworkers, wives and husbands.

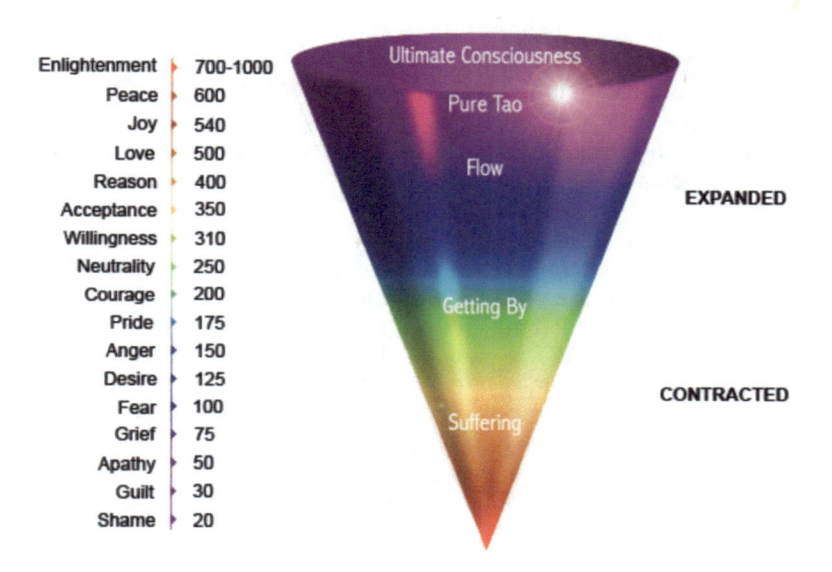

Level	Value
Enlightenment	700-1000
Peace	600
Joy	540
Love	500
Reason	400
Acceptance	350
Willingness	310
Neutrality	250
Courage	200
Pride	175
Anger	150
Desire	125
Fear	100
Grief	75
Apathy	50
Guilt	30
Shame	20

As we draw the curtains in this chapter, we are reminded that transformation knows no boundaries, and its effects are far-reaching. The stories of doctors, lawyers, nurses, and teachers breaking free from the past's chains are a testament to the human capacity for change. Now, it is time to pass this torch to the realm of education. The need for teachers to embark on their own transformative journeys is not just a matter of personal growth; it is a call to action for the betterment of our educational systems, our children, and the world they will shape.

I believe the Ed Matadores mission of revolutionizing the educational system is so important because our teachers are the backbone of the school systems. Relationships and job performance and influence on students are at stake. We are all just operating on a fraction of what is available to us if we don't regulate our subconscious minds and deal with these so-called clogged-up filters.

It's Your Turn Now

I invite you to embark on your own journey. The path to becoming the best version of yourself unleashes the champion within. Now, it's your turn to step into the light. I now run 12-week group coaching programs twice a year, and I host in-person nature retreats to empower you to be the best version of yourself and unleash the champion within that's just waiting to be allowed to come out. We also invite you to join us in the serene embrace of nature during our in-person retreats. Discover the potential you've yet to uncover and join us on this remarkable journey toward becoming your best self. You not only enrich your life but also have the potential to impact the lives of students in all your classrooms.

Challenges I have witnessed in my group coaching programs are mostly centered around my clients not allowing themselves the time or space to thoroughly complete the work of facing their childhood traumas. Not only do they have a difficult time allowing themselves the time needed to complete the work, but I've noticed they also have fear holding them back---fear of what they may find when encountering their silenced inner children whom they have not confronted in decades. I would propose that teachers be given longer breaks within the day to complete the meditations and attend the group coaching calls. Only then will they have a fully regulated reticular activating system and a pure and free subconscious mind.

To implement this initiative of having schools full of completely regulated teachers, we must change how we think about self-care. Self-care does not consist solely of vacations we can't afford, shopping sprees we don't need, and heavy food and alcohol that weigh us down by doing nothing more than numbing us to the problems at hand. Our gestalts are overfilled, and there exists a simple, effective way to empty them and then regulate the emotions within. We must change the narrative of teachers putting themselves last, below their students, families, bosses, and obligations. Teachers need the space to do their own inner work so they can thrive. Teachers, like all of my nurses and doctor clients, need accountability and a belief that they can expect better for themselves. They need a community of like-minded people who are striving to be the best versions of themselves not only for themselves, coworkers, spouses, and their own children but also for their students, whom they have a remarkable influence on.

ED. Matadores

Watch the webinar to understand how your subconscious mind is holding you back by clicking the prompts in the QR code below:

To speak with me to discover the subconscious blocks in your mind, book a free 15 minute call with me by following the prompts in the QR code below:

Cynthia E. Bruton-Thomas

Cynthia Thomas is the owner of Cynthia Thomas Education Consultants (CTE Consultants) and Assistant Professor for the CTE Educator Preparation Department at SUNY Oswego. Cynthia is dedicated to ensuring new educators have a solid pedagogical foundation while developing and implementing career readiness and instructional support for students and marginalized communities. Cynthia has spent many years as a secondary CTE educator and instructional coach. She is currently a doctoral student at The University of Buffalo. Ms. Thomas' company specializes in developing and implementing culturally relevant curricula, professional development, and instructional support. In all of her roles, She has worked to deliver curriculum, teaching methods, and learning experiences that are tailored to the experiences and identities of minority students.

Cultivating Excellence: CTE, DEI, and the Educational Landscape
Cynthia E. Bruton-Thomas:
Owner of CTE Consultants
Assistant Professor: SUNY Oswego

Empowering Futures:
My CTE-DEI Educational Mission
By Cynthia E. Bruton-Thomas

Ed Matadores' mission of revolutionizing education is essential because the need to revitalize teaching is urgent in our rapidly changing world. Traditional educational models often need help to equip students with the skills, knowledge, and mindset required for the complex challenges and opportunities of the 21st century. Revitalizing education involves embracing personalized learning, fostering critical thinking and creativity, promoting cultural awareness and inclusivity, and integrating technology effectively.

My efforts have always been focused on creating and implementing a culturally responsive, career-readiness curriculum that exposes secondary, post-secondary, and adult learners to skills, knowledge, and resources necessary to overcome systemic challenges and contribute to a more diverse and equitable workforce.

Embarking on the CTE Journey

As a CTE educator, I have spent most of my career educating students in urban spaces. I started as an adult educator for various adult career and technical education (CTE) programs, then transitioned to secondary classrooms. This is no coincidence; I am a product of urban education and have been impacted by its parameters.

CTE programming has traditionally included diverse demographics, yet underserved and underrepresented this same population in its efforts for career readiness and access. Historically, urban education has faced challenges such as resource disparities, overcrowded classrooms, and the need to deliver culturally relevant instruction with little to no instruction training or experience. The stigma surrounding CTE and students of color is a persistent challenge that must be addressed. Career and Technical Education pathways have been wrongly perceived as a lesser educational path, perpetuating biases that disproportionately affect students of color. This stigma has hindered students from pursuing CTE opportunities that align with their interests and strengths. By dismantling this stigma and promoting the value of career readiness and culturally responsive instruction, students of color can explore diverse career pathways, acquire practical skills, and succeed in the classroom. Providing a career readiness curriculum aligned with culturally responsive pedagogy is essential to overcoming this obstacle.

Beyond the Classroom: Research Impact in Career and Technical Education

Research supports integrating culturally responsive pedagogy and career readiness initiatives for minority students in Career and Technical Education (CTE) programs. Studies indicate that incorporating culturally relevant content and teaching methods in CTE enhances students' engagement, motivation, and academic achievement. For instance, Ladson-Billings (2009) emphasized that culturally responsive education acknowledges students' backgrounds and provides a more inclusive and practical learning experience.

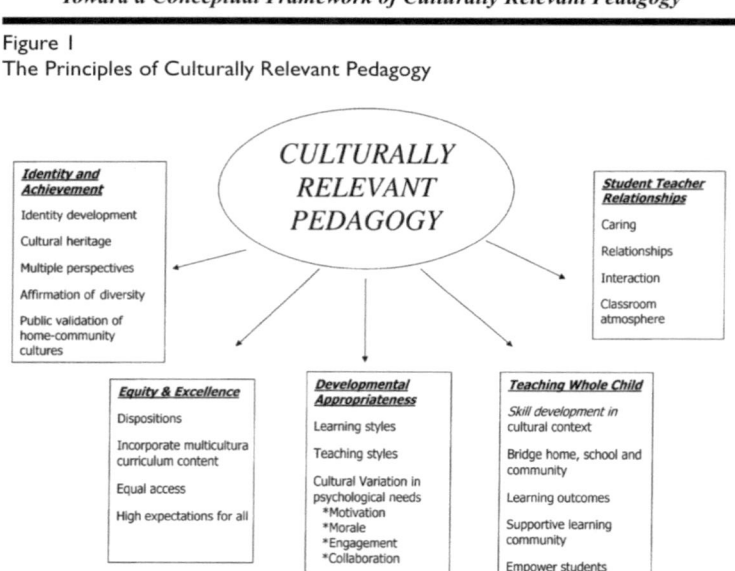

Toward a Conceptual Framework of Culturally Relevant Pedagogy

Figure I
The Principles of Culturally Relevant Pedagogy

CULTURALLY RELEVANT PEDAGOGY

Identity and Achievement
- Identity development
- Cultural heritage
- Multiple perspectives
- Affirmation of diversity
- Public validation of home-community cultures

Student Teacher Relationships
- Caring
- Relationships
- Interaction
- Classroom atmosphere

Equity & Excellence
- Dispositions
- Incorporate multicultural curriculum content
- Equal access
- High expectations for all

Developmental Appropriateness
- Learning styles
- Teaching styles
- Cultural Variation in psychological needs
  - *Motivation
  - *Morale
  - *Engagement
  - *Collaboration

Teaching Whole Child
- Skill development in cultural context
- Bridge home, school and community
- Learning outcomes
- Supportive learning community
- Empower students

Additionally, research by Sleeter and Grant (1999) highlights that culturally relevant curriculum increases students' self-esteem, self-efficacy, and overall success. The work of Pinder (2017) underscores that connecting CTE with culturally meaningful career pathways improves minority students' career exploration and preparation.

Systemic changes to implement culturally responsive pedagogy and career readiness in CTE should encompass teacher training in culturally competent teaching strategies, curriculum revision to include diverse perspectives, equitable resource allocation, culturally inclusive career counseling, and addressing systemic educational inequalities (Gay, 2018; Ladson-Billings, 2009).

Collaborative efforts among educators, administrators, policymakers, and communities are pivotal in establishing an inclusive educational environment that fosters minority students' success in CTE (Ladson-Billings, 2009; Pinder, 2017).

The positive impact of integrating career readiness and culturally responsive instruction in CTE yields many benefits and transformative outcomes. By intertwining career readiness principles, students not only acquire practical skills and industry-specific knowledge but also have a deep understanding of the professional world and the part they play in it.

Forward Thinking in CTE Programs

Career and Technical Education have identified many growth opportunities due to the COVID-19 pandemic. Limited program opportunities, limited college and career preparedness, lack of skills training, teacher shortages, and equity issues are significant concerns within the field. I have always focused on providing educational access and opportunity for marginalized communities through culturally responsive instructional practices and career readiness.

Implementing culturally responsive instruction ensures that education is tailored to honor and embrace students' diverse cultural backgrounds and identities.

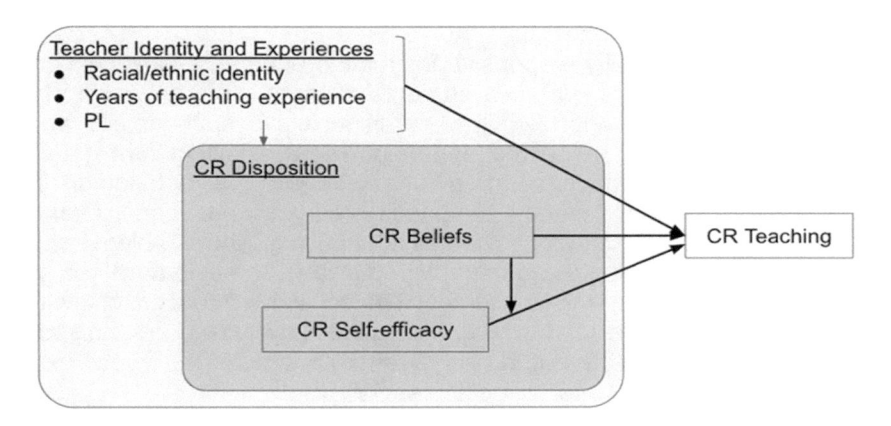

Teacher Identity and Experiences
- Racial/ethnic identity
- Years of teaching experience
- PL

CR Disposition
- CR Beliefs
- CR Self-efficacy

→ CR Teaching

This approach fosters an inclusive environment where students feel valued, respected, and empowered, resulting in heightened engagement, motivation, and a strong sense of belonging. The connection between career readiness and cultural responsiveness nurtures students' self-efficacy, critical thinking, and problem-solving abilities, ultimately equipping them with the tools to navigate a complex global workforce with artistic acumen. The collective impact is cultivating well-rounded, culturally aware, and career-ready individuals poised to excel in diverse professional fields and contribute positively to an inclusive and globally interconnected society.

Rethinking Paradigms: Catalysts for Change in CTE

Implementing culturally responsive career readiness experiences is an ongoing process in Career and Technical Education (CTE) because it reflects the dynamic nature of education and the evolving needs of students and society. Cultural responsiveness requires continuous adaptation to the changing demographics, diverse identities, and evolving industries. By consistently refining and expanding culturally responsive career readiness experiences, CTE programs can ensure they remain relevant, effective, and impactful in preparing students for the ever-changing global landscape.

Collaboration and input from various stakeholders are also necessary for culturally responsive career readiness. Educators, administrators, students, parents, and community leaders are essential participants. Educators drive curriculum delivery, administrators provide resources and support, and students offer insights into their cultural backgrounds and learning needs. Parents' involvement ensures cultural sensitivity and community leaders contribute to contextual relevance. This collaborative effort ensures the curriculum aligns with diverse perspectives, creating an inclusive and practical educational experience.

Implementing culturally responsive instruction ensures that education is tailored to honor and embrace students' diverse cultural backgrounds and identities. This approach fosters an inclusive environment where students feel valued, respected, and empowered, resulting in heightened engagement, motivation, and a strong sense of belonging. The connection between career readiness and cultural responsiveness nurtures students' self-efficacy, critical thinking, and problem-solving abilities, ultimately equipping them with the tools to navigate a complex global workforce with artistic acumen. The collective impact is cultivating well-rounded, culturally aware, and career-ready individuals poised to excel in diverse professional fields and contribute positively to an inclusive and globally interconnected society.

From Passion to Action: My Involvement in CTE Excellence

Integrating career readiness with culturally responsive teaching is essential to creating a holistic educational experience that equips students with practical skills and recognizes and values their diverse backgrounds, fostering inclusivity, motivation, and success. I've coached novice CTE educators on pedagogical best practices needed to be effective in their instruction while aligning with the needs of diverse learners(culturally responsive teaching). My personal and professional experiences created a space for me to love educating learners who reflect me. Before my work, students were only taught career readiness through a non-diverse lens. Representation in staff, curriculum, and learning experience needed to be addressed. Aligning career readiness instruction to honor marginalized students, cultural backgrounds, and views was a practice that must be prioritized more cohesively.

My efforts address this need by creating instructional tools, curricula, and learning experiences centered around sustainable career readiness/ culturally responsive instructional content. I work to identify or create a curriculum aligned with learning standards and address career readiness while reflecting on students' experiences. This creates an environment of learning that is not only student-centered but represents diversity within the learning community. The teaching experiences center around self-expression & efficacy with learning from others with diverse perspectives. In this approach, students engage in instruction that meets their cultural needs and prepares them with the skills needed to succeed in all facets of life.

Integrating career readiness and culturally responsive teaching in CTE is crucial to addressing the evolving needs of students and the demands of a diverse and global workforce. By aligning and implementing a solution for career readiness and culturally responsive teaching, students are better prepared to navigate professional settings, communicate across various contexts, and contribute meaningfully to their chosen fields.

My latest endeavor involves researching and creating an instructional framework that identifies fundamental principles and strategies that career and technical education teachers need to implement culturally responsive and sustaining teaching practices effectively. Within this framework, there will be implementation strategies for all CTE educators to increase student engagement, improve academic performance, and create an inclusive and empowering learning environment that values diverse perspectives and backgrounds. This framework ensures educators develop the cultural competence and awareness necessary for student success.

Disruptive Change: The Call to Revolutionize

CTE instruction and opportunities have shaped my career as a CTE professional. Early exposure to the career readiness curriculum, combined with my extensive experience in the cosmetology industry, has given me a profound understanding and appreciation for the value of this content. As a black woman in the field, I recognize the crucial importance of aligning and exposing students of color to diverse career pathways and employability skills. This effort aims to break down historical barriers, promote equitable education, and facilitate career advancement.

Recognizing and addressing issues within CTE is paramount for optimizing student outcomes. By focusing on key areas of improvement, we can enhance the overall effectiveness of CTE programs. Key considerations include:
- Systemic changes are imperative to effectively implement culturally responsive pedagogy and career readiness for minority students in CTE.
- Teacher preparation programs should incorporate training in culturally competent teaching practices.
- School districts and educational institutions need to evaluate and revise curricula to ensure the representation of diverse cultures and experiences.
- Adequate funding should be allocated to provide updated resources, modern equipment, and technology across all CTE programs.
- Culturally inclusive career counseling and mentorship programs must be established to guide students toward pathways that align with their interests and cultural backgrounds.
- Addressing systemic inequities in educational funding, opportunities, and access to advanced courses is crucial.
- Planning and considering students' needs is a critical step that, if overlooked, can directly impact sustainability.
- Educational institutions should create a career readiness curriculum that equips students with practical skills and fosters cultural awareness, inclusivity, and respect for diverse identities.
- Defining the organization's objectives is essential because it clearly outlines the goals and learning outcomes you aim to achieve. Curriculum development and cultural awareness were assessed, clearly identifying the need for professional development surrounding the content and integrating culturally responsive practices within the content.

Ultimately, tackling challenges within CTE is not just about resolving immediate issues; it is an investment in each student's success, growth, and future achievements, paving the way for enriched educational experiences and positive outcomes.

ED. Matadores

Offer: Free 30-Minute Discovery Call

This complimentary 30-minute discovery call and DEI professional development guide are designed to align career readiness and DEI practices within your school, district, or CTE organization. We will explore potential solutions to provide your organization with valuable curriculum insights, professional development solutions, and career readiness services, enhancing your CTE program. This personalized approach ensures that your specific career readiness and DEI needs align with industry requirements, ultimately contributing to student success.

Contact us via email today to schedule your session.

Bio & Connect with Me: Cynthia Thomas

ED. Matadores

EQUITABLE SCHOOL MODELS

Dr. Donna Vallese
Education Leader & CEO of Inspiring Leaders, LLC

Dr. Donna Vallese has been an educator for over 2 decades, is a TEDx and international speaker, an international bestselling author, and awardee of the 2023 Education 2.0 Visionaries and the 2022 Education 2.0 Outstanding Leadership Award. She is a school district leader and is also the CEO of Inspiring Leaders LLC. Work for Dr. Donna has always been focused on innovative practices that transform the educational system to create equity for children so that they can reach their fullest potential. She coaches leaders and currently is building a collective of innovators in education. This collective aims to revolutionize the educational system through a series of books, memberships, and conferences.

Join my mailing list:
https://inspiringleaders.network/

Competency-Based Grading For Equitable Learning
By Dr. Donna Vallese

Reflecting on Grades

Have you ever considered what a grade means? What does 83% mean? Did you get 17% of your answers wrong? Did you turn your paper in late? Did you make some grammatical errors? Feedback is often limited, and the final number seems arbitrary.

In a 100-point grading system, the first 64 points are a failing grade, the next 5 points are equivalent to a D, a C and B are each worth 10 points, and an A worth 11 points. The educational system says most people should fall within a C average, but really the expectation is that successful students hold A's and B's. Statistically, these numbers do not work.

As a student, I was motivated by grades, but not all students are like that. I have had many students whose potential I could see, but they just did not have the same motivation for grades that I did. When I became a mom, my son hated school and did not care what grades he received, no matter how much his achievements were rewarded. He struggled to keep himself organized, so while he would complete assignments, he would forget to turn them in and lose them. I watched his academic confidence drastically decline over the course of his school career, despite his obvious high intellect and ability.

Questioning Traditional Grading

My son's teachers struggled to understand why I pushed back on them, asking questions such as "What are you grading? Timeliness or conceptual understanding?" Of course, the answer was typically understanding, but he was being penalized for timeliness and organization.

A 100-point grading scale is a high-stakes system that does not accurately measure ability, yet we use it to place students into tracks that determine their futures. There are a few exceptions where some schools have shifted to competency-based grading with a 4 or 5 point scale. These alternative approaches allow teachers to more accurately assess students' abilities and cultivate areas of growth. When applied correctly, this type of grading can also become internal motivators for the students as they begin to see the purpose of their learning and are better able to focus on what areas where growth is needed most.

Assessing Competency

Is it more important that students memorize information or is it more important that they learn the skills they need to be successful members of our society? How we grade students plays a big role in defining where the focus is in the classroom. Therefore, changing the model of how we grade requires that teaching becomes more focused on building competence rather than memorization, which better meets the purpose of education.

For over two decades, my career has afforded me many opportunities to teach and grade students using non-traditional methods. As a teacher, I focused on project-based learning and graded students' skills in each assignment on a 4-point scale. Students were actively engaged and interested in their own progress.

Competency-based grading focuses on measuring students' proficiency of skills rather than simply passing assessments, tests, homework completion, and timeliness. Competencies are typically skills that are applied across all content areas. While content is important and can also be graded, the emphasis is on the demonstration of skill mastery that benefits students for a lifetime.

Some examples of competencies are as follows:
- Effectively communicating ideas and information in all communication forms.
- Applying the scientific method and critical thinking to investigate natural phenomena.
- Applying mathematical concepts to solve real-world problems.
- Demonstrating an understanding of diverse cultures, their histories, and their impact on society.
- Effectively evaluating and navigating digital technologies for various purposes.

Competencies provide a clear framework for assessing student mastery and can be tailored to the unique requirements of each subject. An assignment given to students may have multiple grades assigned to it that are based on the specific skills being assessed; with each skill being worth 3-5 points.

With competency-based grading, educators assess skill development over time, rather than through finite assignments. This means that students have multiple opportunities to demonstrate learning and mastery. The need to give a 0 becomes unnecessary unless absolutely no work is ever turned in.

Impact of Grading Strategies

In traditional grading it is nearly impossible for a student to overcome a 0. This demonstrates that a traditional grade is not an accurate representation of a student's abilities. The chart below demonstrates how a 0 affects a student's grade average across three assignments, using three different grading approaches. For each column, assume that each of the three assignments is the same. For simplicity, only 0's and 100's have been used and all have been equally weighted.

Chart: Traditional v. Competency-Based Grading

100-Point Traditional Grading System	100-Point Grading System with Timeliness Graded Separately	Competency-Based Grading System With 4-Point Rubrics
Assignment Score Assignment 1 - 0 Assignment 2 - 100 Assignment 3 - 100	Assignment Score Assignment 1 - 100 Timeliness - 0 Assignment 2 - 100 Timeliness - 100 Assignment 3 - 100 Timeliness - 100	Assignment Score Assign 1 - Skill 1 - 0 Assign 1 - Skill 2 - 4 Assign 1 - Skill 3 - 4 Assign 2 - Skill 1 - 4 Assign 2 - Skill 2 - 4 Assign 2 - Skill 3 - 4 Assign 3 - Skill 1 - 4 Assign 3 - Skill 2 - 4 Assign 3 - Skill 3 - 4
Average = 66.6%	Average = 83.3%	Average = 3.6 Average = 90%

The first column demonstrates a traditional 100-point grading system. With three assignments all weighted evenly, if a student turned in Assignment 1 too late to be given credit, the highest average that student could receive is a 66.7%, or a D. Given that the other two grades are 100, it easily demonstrates that the D is not a good representation of that student's abilities.

In the middle column, each assignment is given two grades: one based on content and one for timeliness. If the student turned in Assignment 1 too late to be given credit, at least the learning has been graded. However, given the other high grades, the average of 83.3% (a B) is also not a good representation of ability.

The last column demonstrates how competency-based grading could be used. Each skill is graded on a 4-point scale for each assignment. In this example, there are three skills graded for each of the three assignments. Now we can see that skill 1 needs some work, but the other skills have been given the highest score possible. The average in this model is 3.6, which translates to 90%. Because of the diagnostic nature of this approach and the specificity attached to each grade, the final score is likely much more representative of the student's abilities.

Benefits of Competency-Based Grading

In addition to better-representing students' skills, competency-based grading offers several other advantages:
- Rubrics provide clear criteria that help students understand what to do to demonstrate mastery, set goals, and facilitate specific feedback for learning.
- There are opportunities for students to progress at their own pace rather than all being simultaneously at the same level, which is counterproductive to learning and not realistic.
- By focusing on learning rather than completion of assignments, students have opportunities to develop a deeper understanding of content which aids in effective retention and application.
- Students' engagement and motivation increases because their grading is focused on lifelong skills with real-world value.
- Achievement gaps are reduced because strengths and areas of growth are more accurately tracked to provide customized instruction to better support learning.

Furthermore, competency-based grading provides a much more equitable approach to grading because barriers to finding success are removed for students who need them to be removed. Students who excel are also able to continue to further develop their abilities rather than being held back by their peers, thus allowing them to achieve beyond what was believed possible.

Competency-Based Grading in Practice

While the number of schools has gradually increased in the use of competency-based grading, it is still rare to find an educator who has experience with it. A few years ago, in the urban district I worked in, our guest presenter on equity in schools asked the audience of 125 administrators who had experience with competency-based grading. Only two of us raised our hands.

I have had the privilege of leading two different public charter high schools that implemented competency-based grading. These experiences were powerful for me as well as for the students. For instance, one day a concerned parent came to me about her daughter's struggles in school. This student was intelligent, worked for hours on her homework every night, yet was still not getting the results she was striving hard for. I pulled out this student's grades and report card. We noticed that across every subject the student's grades for understanding the content, critical thinking, collaboration, reading comprehension, and other key skills all demonstrated proficiency or mastery. All except for one skill area... writing. Her writing grades were low in every class. This realization allowed me to work with each of her teachers to develop plans to focus on improving her writing skills in all areas. Within a few months, this student was able to improve her writing skills, confidence, and grades.

Why Schools Do Not Adopt Competency-Based Grading

Despite the many benefits of competency-based grading, this approach is still rare in our schools. Some of the contributing factors are:
- Transitioning to competency-based grading is a complex process that involves redefining curriculum, assessments, and teaching methods
- Shifting the culture of the school and all stakeholders who experienced education the traditional way.
- The heavy emphasis on standardized testing for accountability that focuses on memorization.
- Time and funding needed for providing professional development, appropriate technology platforms and time to calibrate grading for equity and consistency.
- A lack of consistency across institutions making it difficult to compare students' achievements or transfer credits between schools.

However, these challenges are surmountable, and the benefits of competency-based grading outweigh the time, effort, and expense required.

Revolutionizing Education

Revolutionizing our educational system's grading method is entirely possible but requires pushing for change at several levels, including policy, curriculum, teacher training, and cultural attitudes toward education.

Some key considerations include:
- Stakeholders—including parents—who should be educated about the benefits of competency-based grading to gain their advocacy.
- Education policies and regulations at the district, state, and national levels should be updated, and guidelines should be developed to encourage consistent, rigorous, and equitable competency-based grading practices.
- Competency-based grading should be aligned with the expectations of colleges, universities, and employers so that students are well-prepared for post-secondary education and the workforce.

- Developing flexible, student-centered curriculum structures that allow students to set and monitor their own learning goals, progress at their own pace, and include options for acceleration and additional support.
- Teachers should be provided with professional development to develop an understanding of competency-based grading and design appropriate assessments for students to demonstrate their understanding and skills.

Implementing competency-based grading in schools requires a collaborative effort among educators, administrators, policymakers, parents, and the broader community. If executed broadly and effectively, it would be revolutionary in our educational system with profound benefits to our students.

Timothy Andrew Smith, Ed.D.
CEO

Timothy Andrew Smith is the founder and CEO of Learning Matters Educational Group (LMEG) a leading charter school management organization. Timothy founded ThrivePoint High Schools and Calibre Academy in Arizona and Taylion High Desert Academy in San Bernardino County, California. LMEG has been working with charter schools for over 25 years serving 1800 students in Arizona and 800 students in California. LMEG is growing with plans to open new charter schools in Nevada, Utah, Oklahoma and Texas over the next three years. Timothy has a Global Executive EdD. In Educational Leadership from the University of Southern California and a Global MBA from the Thunderbird School of Global Management.

Bridging The Achievement Gap With An Innovative Blended Learning Model
By Timothy Andrew Smith, Ed.D.

ThrivePoint High School (TPHS) is a public charter school network that is designed to serve students at-risk of dropping out, who are over-aged and under-credited, and who do not work well in a traditional environment. TPHS started in 2000, offering digital learning before online schools became popular. We serve over 1,300 students with online and flex-blended learning across six resource centers in Arizona.

As the founder and CEO of Learning Matters Educational Group, a charter school management company that works with schools in Arizona and California, I have been leading and operating TPHS since its inception. TPHS was not the first charter school model that I started. Our first charter school was the International Studies Academy (ISA). This school was a success from the beginning. However, we found that we were only reaching a limited number of students who met the enrollment criteria. We were turning away many students who were looking for a flexible charter school option. We realized that there was a bigger opportunity helping at-risk students with an innovative alternative high school model.

ED. Matadores

The Ed Matadores mission of revolutionizing the educational system is critically important. The public school system still uses a rigid and outdated factory model first developed over 100 years ago. Even now, the public school system expects students to learn from a traditional, one-size-fits-all seat-based model. Many public school teachers still lecture to students as a sage on the stage, leaving many students behind for the sake of covering content regardless of assessing individual student needs. Meanwhile, an increasing number of students exercise the only school choice option available to them by dropping out of school, leaving themselves alone to take on family and job responsibilities without a high school diploma.

The problem with traditional education is that students who fall behind are not able to catch up with their peers. Schools require students to take six classes in a semester format that does not allow for credit recovery or credit acceleration. TPHS uses a flexible learning model where students take two courses for six weeks. This enables students to get on track to graduation or, in some cases, accelerate their learning and graduate early. TPHS's flexible mastery-based learning model has helped many students who had given up on traditional school. Many TPHS students believed that they couldn't learn when it was really the rigid educational environment that caused them to fail.

Three Pillars to Success

As part of TPHS's new model, the team identified the three pillars of Enrollment, Engagement, and Achievement, with goals and Key Performance Indicators (KPIs) for each. These goals and KPIs gave us a roadmap as we worked to improve performance in each area.

The first pillar of Enrollment was monitored by the growth of our student body. Prior to the pandemic, with some of the more traditional practices in place, TPHS's enrollment was dropping at some campuses. Therefore, TPHS's leadership shifted their model to reverse the decline. As of November 2023, TPHS has exceeded 1,300 students and is on track to exceed 1,600 students by the end of the year.

TPHS's second pillar is Engagement. We measure engagement by monitoring the number of credits that students earn while at school. Many students come to TPHS behind in credits, some as much as one to two years behind their peers. TPHS's model allows students to earn credits at an accelerated rate. After implementing the new strategies, our engagement rate increased, with nearly 90% of students earning more than one year's worth of credits within a year's time.

TPHS's third pillar is Achievement. Our innovative alternative model allows at-risk students to experience academic success, and become college and career-ready. We use the Arizona Alternative Academic Framework that our leadership helped design with many other Arizona stakeholders. This framework defines the success of an alternative education school by measuring credits earned, the percentage of students on track to graduate, and indicators of college and career readiness.

The ThrivePoint Story: A Research-based Solution

Our schools are successful because we implement multiple high impactful and innovative strategies simultaneously. It has taken more than three years to get to this point and has been a journey that other schools and districts can learn from.

Small Schools

TPHS sees a small school model as critical to the success of at-risk students. A study of 68 small non-selective high schools in New York City found that school leadership quality, teacher empowerment, teacher mutual support, personalized learning, and teacher/student respect were promising levers for increasing graduation rates for disadvantaged students (Bloom, Unterman, Zhu & Reardon, 2020). Large-scale studies comparing student performance in large and small schools have consistently found that small schools improve student achievement, especially the performance of disadvantaged students. In small schools, minority and lower-achieving students seem to do better, as marginal or at-risk students are much more likely to become involved, to make an effort, and to achieve. Small schools are far more likely to be violence-free, have better-behaved students, and have fewer students drop out (Raywid, 1998).

Mastery-based Learning

TPHS operated for many years in a blended learning no-man's land, not fitting into either the brick-and-mortar environment or with fully online schools. This disconnect is due to external factors from state authorizers, accrediting bodies, and traditional operators unwilling to think outside the traditional school box.

Due to external barriers, TPHS offered a combination of two digital classes along with two traditional instructor-led classes for several years. Digital classes allowed students to learn in a mastery-based format, recovering lost credits by showing at least a 70% mastery level. Mastery-based learning has been shown to help students improve their academic self-concept, stay on task, and develop a growth mindset (Anderson, 1994; Duby, 1981; Dweck, 2006; Guskey & Pigott, 1988). Students using mastery-based learning are more satisfied with the instruction they receive and have more positive attitudes toward the content they are learning compared to students in traditional classes (Anderson, 1994; Kulik, Kulik, & Bangert-Drowns, 1990). With this mastery-based format, students were able to move on to the next course in real-time rather than wait for their teacher's schedule. Students can now catch up and get on track to graduate.

Short Intensive Learning Periods

TPHS operates on six-week learning periods with students working intensively on two courses at a time. This change from a semester-based model to six-week courses allowed students to have additional flexibility. Students are better able to accelerate their learning to catch up or move ahead in classes if desired. Students can also extend classes for an additional six weeks if needed. Shorter intensive learning periods have been used successfully in higher education for several years and have proven to be a successful methodology for effective credit recovery (Durdella & Durdella, 2009; Geltner & Ruth, 2001; Holzweiss, Polnick & Lunenburg, 2019).

Alternative Attendance Tracking

Fortunately, the Covid-19 pandemic shut down forced state authorizers to re-evaluate how to monitor online and blended learning schools. The pandemic also forced TPHS to consider using alternative strategies to better serve our students.

The State of Arizona passed new legislation called Instructional Time Model (ITM). This allowed Arizona schools to determine their own method of collecting student attendance data. This new funding mechanism was a game changer for TPHS, allowing us to eliminate the outdated seat time model. We could take full advantage of flexible mastery-based learning. Our teachers could work with students in a small group learning environment without being hindered by monitoring classroom time. Students could come to school, work with their teachers in a small group environment, get assistance on specific concepts, and work on their online classes.

Student Success Coaching

TPHS knew that part of its innovative model was the personalized connection that students had to their teachers and staff. Therefore, TPHS looked to higher education best practices for innovation and implemented a Student Success Coach (SSC) model at each campus and online. The idea behind the coach is to be a support and mentor to online students to help them stay organized and engaged in their online classes. The SSC is not a teaching position, since each student has online teachers with whom they interact on a regular basis. SSCs stay with the students throughout their academic journey. In addition to assisting students with their courses, coaches also support them with personal matters that could be barriers to active involvement in school.

Orienting Students for a New Way of Learning

TPHS designed the ThrivePoint Vibe course. This course introduces students to online learning and helps them identify their learning style, and become more organized and self-directed in their learning. The Vibe course helps students—particularly those with anxiety about school—to increase their self-confidence in learning. TPHS teachers and coaches help students chunk their learning into manageable bites for quick wins, with support to help them celebrate success.

The Call for Revolution

TPHS has been able to provide an innovative and flexible learning option for at-risk students to be successful in school and ready for careers and college. There are many systemic obstacles that prevent an innovative program such as TPHS to be replicated on a larger scale.

One roadblock to implementing innovation in schools is in allowing for more school choice or charter school options in each state. Some states still do not have charter legislation and many states have a cap on the number of charter schools that they approve each year. In addition to improving charter school access, states need to review their current online or blended learning attendance models. Many people have concluded that online learning does not work since it was implemented so poorly during the Pandemic. Online and blended learning has proven to be successful in higher education if implemented thoughtfully and properly. States need to allow schools the flexibility to implement new technologies, resources and educational practices in a manner that can be effectively launched to increase educational innovation and reform.

Finally, at national, state, and local levels, educational policy makers need to address the academic achievement gap and design schools and programs that meet the needs of at-risk students. Schools must be smaller, more adaptable, more flexible, and more relevant to the needs of today's marginalized youth. Schools should include mastery-based learning, career training and personalized learning plans to help our youth to become more engaged in school.

ED. Matadores

Timothy Andrew Smith will be starting a new blog at www.flexiblelearning.org Please sign in to get updates on research and best practices in the field of flexible learning.

Follow Me On Social Media:
https://blinq.me/witAs98gZKVz?bs=db
https://www.linkedin.com/in/timothy-smith-7162b02a/
https://www.facebook.com/ThrivePointHS
www.learningmatters.org

ED. Matadores

Ioanna Mantzouridou Onasi
Co-founder & CEO of Dextego

Ioanna Mantzouridou Onasi, Co-founder and CEO of Dextego is an AI Coach for Soft Skills Development. Since its launch in June 2023, her platform has gained remarkable traction from solopreneurs, growth startups, and enterprises. Her academic and work background as Vice President (VP) of People and Chief of Staff at Aptivio, a VC-backed B2B SaaS startup specializing in Revenue AI has given her valuable insights into the goals and challenges of Human Resources and Talent Development Professionals. Fundamentally, these goals include attracting and retaining top talent. But the most fundamental challenge is skill development.

Redefining Education For The Future: The Power Of Soft Skills
By Ioanna Mantzouridou Onasi

According to PWC, over 80% of CEOs understand that the skills gap threatens their organizations. To help companies achieve their goals, Ioanna co-founded Dextego with Sean Vazquez. Dextego's AI Coaching Platform offers personalized, bite-sized and on-demand soft skills training. Users practice scenario-based challenges and get personalized feedback based on their facial expressions, tone, pitch, and content of what they say. They created an Emotion Engine to understand human emotion.

Bridging the Gap Between Classroom Learning and Workplace Success

This chapter explores the vital importance of soft skills in shaping high-performing individuals and advocates for their integration into educational systems to bridge the gap between classroom learning and workplace success. In the past, education primarily focused on academic subjects to impart knowledge and expertise in specific domains. However, the employment landscape has shifted dramatically, and employers now seek more than technical know-how. Soft skills, encompassing communication, teamwork, adaptability, problem-solving, emotional intelligence, and more increasingly valued by employers as they contribute to overall workplace efficiency and productivity. These skills are not easily replaceable by automation and artificial intelligence, making them essential for future-proofing careers.

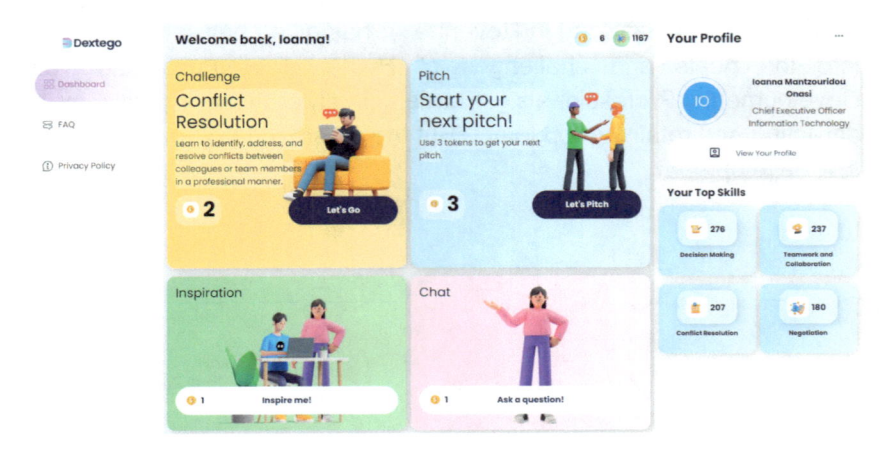

Attracting A players in this competitive job market is very challenging. According to Paychex, Inc. (2023), larger businesses (20-plus employees) use training as the top tactic to attract Gen Z workers (ages 18-26). Additionally, studies have shown that soft skills significantly boost productivity and retention with a remarkable 12% increase, leading to a 2.5x return on investment. Dextego addresses the problem of a need for soft skills by fast-tracking career advancement through soft skills training, such as enhancing effective communication, cultivating leadership skills, and elevating pitching and public speaking skills. It equips young professionals with the necessary skills and knowledge to excel in their roles, showcasing their continuous learning and development. LinkedIn research has found that 89% of bad hires are due to a lack of soft skills. With hyper-personalization, gamified learning, and actionable feedback, Dextego offers a human-centric approach to developing soft skills applicable to Gen Z employees across all industries, preparing them for the future of work. Gen Z employees are digital natives and learn differently; they want micro-learning and engagement more than any other generation. AI doesn't just fill skill gaps; it democratizes learning. With AI-powered platforms, we see personalized training paths, offering equal opportunities regardless of one's background or location. It's about understanding and catering to individual learning styles, bringing equitable access to career development.

The Urgent Need for Educational Reform

The need for educational reform has become evident as the disconnect between traditional academic learning and real-world application widens, leading to a war for talent. By incorporating soft skills into the curriculum, educators can provide students with a comprehensive toolkit that prepares them for the challenges of the modern workforce. Instead of solely focusing on rote memorization and standardized testing, educational institutions must prioritize nurturing qualities. One of the significant advantages of integrating soft skills into education is the seamless transition of students into the workplace. Students with strong communication skills can articulate their ideas effectively, sell themselves more easily in an interview, collaborate with others, and lead teams efficiently. Problem-solving skills enable them to tackle real-world challenges, and emotional intelligence empowers them to handle interpersonal dynamics with empathy and understanding. These attributes create a highly skilled workforce adaptable to evolving business environments. As the job market grows, there is an urgent need for education to adapt accordingly.

ED. Matadores

Preparing Students for the Demands of the Future Workforce

The digital age has ushered in an era of innovation and automation, significantly impacting the jobs available. Routine tasks are increasingly automated, emphasizing uniquely human qualities—soft skills. As technology reshapes industries, the ability to adapt, communicate, and collaborate becomes indispensable for success. To prepare students for the demands of the future workforce, educational institutions must embrace a more holistic approach to learning. There is a need to revise the curriculum to incorporate interdisciplinary studies, project-based learning, and real-world simulations. By providing students with opportunities to apply their knowledge in practical scenarios, they can develop problem-solving skills and gain insights into the complexities of the professional world. Technology can be pivotal in fostering soft skills if used wisely.

Balancing Technology and Human Interaction

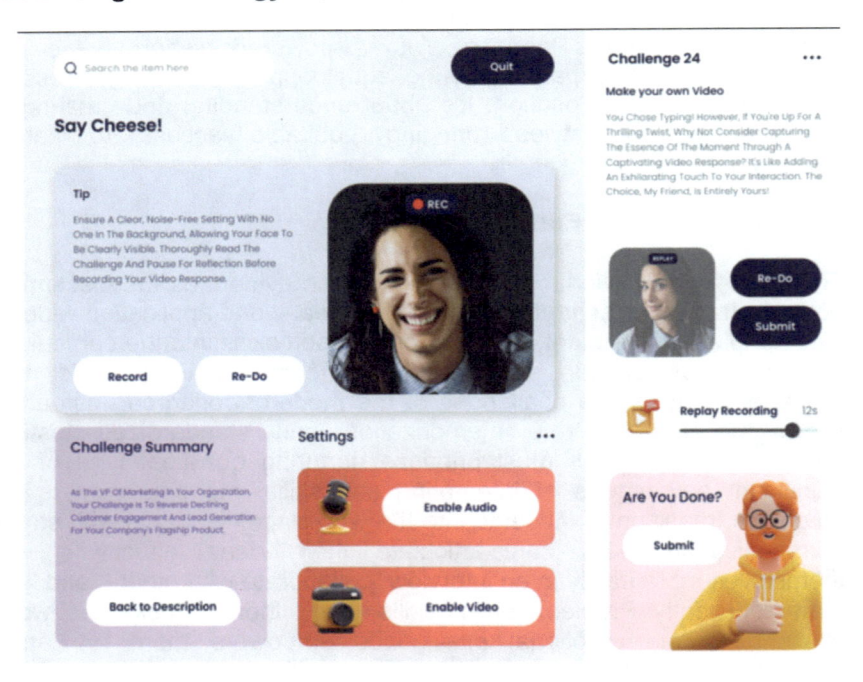

Dextego's AI Coach offers daily personalized micro-challenges to prepare students for their future careers. However, it is essential to strike a balance, ensuring that technology complements and enhances the development of soft skills rather than replacing human interaction. Educators must receive adequate training and professional development to revolutionize education for the future workforce. Schools and universities should invest in programs that equip teachers with the knowledge and skills necessary to effectively incorporate soft skills development into their teaching methods. Additionally, partnerships between academia and industry can facilitate a better understanding of the skills needed in the job market, enabling educators to tailor their approaches accordingly.

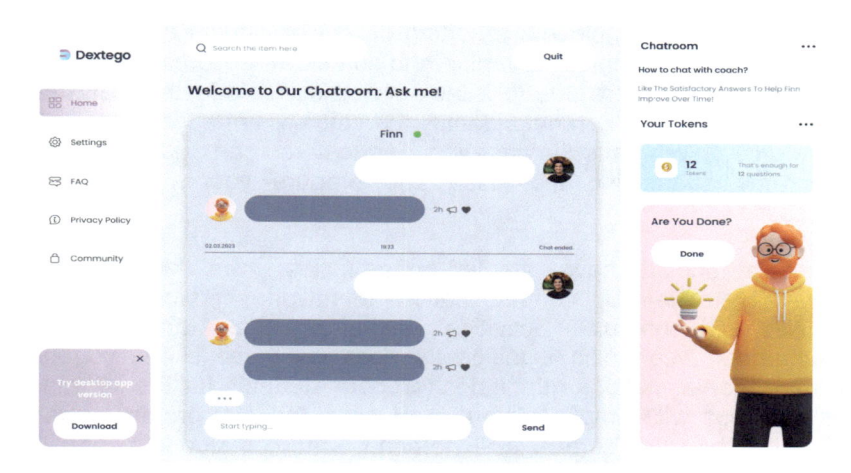

The Role of Policymakers in Shaping Education

For meaningful change, policymakers must recognize the importance of soft skills in education and establish frameworks that promote integration in the curricula. Funding initiatives, policy guidelines, and collaboration between governments, businesses, and educational institutions can facilitate the implementation of soft skills development programs. Policymakers can foster a more competitive and resilient workforce by creating an environment that values and prioritizes these skills. Apart from the financial means, the transition to emphasizing soft skills requires a cultural shift in educational institutions. Encouraging a growth mindset that values continuous learning, resilience, and adaptability can empower students to embrace challenges and develop their soft skills with enthusiasm. Teachers and mentors play a crucial role in fostering this mindset by providing constructive feedback and creating a supportive learning environment.

Lifelong Learning and Skill Development

Education should not be confined to a specific phase of life; instead, it must become a lifelong pursuit. As the job market evolves, individuals must continuously update their skills to remain relevant and competitive. Educational institutions should promote lifelong learning opportunities and provide resources to help graduates refine their soft skills throughout their careers. The widening skills gap has become a critical issue with many employers reporting difficulties finding candidates with the right mix of technical expertise and soft skills. According to LinkedIn, 89% of bad hires are due to a lack of soft skills. Industry analysis and employer feedback can help identify the soft skills needed in the current workforce. With this information, educators can design targeted programs addressing the issue and prepare young graduates for success.

Students should have ample opportunities from kindergarten to university to develop communication, teamwork, and problem-solving abilities. Co-curricular activities, such as clubs and community engagement, can also significantly enhance these skills. To ensure educational institutions adequately prepare students for the job market, partnerships with employers are invaluable. Industry professionals can offer insights into current skill demands, mentor students, and even provide internships or apprenticeships that offer hands-on experience in the real world. Dextego's AI Coach provides personalized feedback on what skills students and professionals need to further develop. Such feedback can help refine educational approaches and create a feedback loop between educators and employers.

Rethinking Educational Assessments

Beyond their professional benefits, soft skills contribute significantly to personal growth and well-being. Emotional intelligence enhances self-awareness and empathy, fostering better relationships and mental resilience. Creative thinking and problem-solving skills enable individuals to approach challenges with ingenuity and confidence. By prioritizing the development of soft skills, education can empower students to lead fulfilling and purpose-driven lives. Cultural competence and inclusivity are crucial aspects of soft skills development as well. Educators must acknowledge and embrace the diversity of perspectives and experiences in their classrooms. By creating an inclusive learning environment, students can enhance their communication and teamwork skills while gaining a broader understanding of the world. Lastly, there is a need for a holistic approach to educational assessments to evolve into recognizing the value of soft skills. Standardized testing often fails to capture the complexity of these skills. Holistic assessment methods, such as portfolio reviews, project evaluations, and behavioral interviews, in combination with Dextego's personalized reports, can provide a more comprehensive view of a student's soft skills development.

Preparing for a Brighter Future

In conclusion, integrating soft skills into education is a beneficial addition and an essential transformation to prepare individuals for a future of uncertainty and rapid change. By rethinking the role of education and prioritizing the cultivation of soft skills, we can unlock the potential of each student and empower them to thrive in the workplace and beyond. Embracing this shift is not just a matter of adapting to the changing job market but a recognition of the intrinsic value of developing well-rounded individuals who can positively impact society. As educators, policymakers, and stakeholders come together to embrace the soft skills, we lay the foundation for a brighter, more adaptable, and more resilient future. Ed Matadores' mission of revolutionizing the educational system is so important because the future of work depends on the future of education. In less than a year, the feedback about Dextego has been overwhelmingly positive, but this is just the beginning. Our mission for large-scale impact is for all students to have access to Dextego's AI Coach to prepare for the workforce by completing personalized challenges adapted to their career path and having access to an AI Coach 24/7.

Use code DEXTER1000 for a free month of Dextego

If you want to develop your soft skills via a personalized and unbiased 24/7 AI Coach scand this QR Code:

Read more at https://dextego.com/

Contact Me on Linkedin:
https://www.linkedin.com/in/joannemantzouridou/

Catalyzing Change: Uniting Leaders for a Transformative Educational Future
By María Angélica Benavides, Ed.D.

In conclusion, the Ed Matadores collective serves as a powerful testament to the resilience and innovation of educational leaders nationwide. From school principals breaking through boundaries to district officials championing systemic change, the narratives shared illuminate the transformative efforts within our educational landscape.

These stories emphasize the critical need to identify and dismantle unnecessary constraints embedded in the system. District leaders, including superintendents and directors, play a pivotal role in fostering an environment where success is not hindered by outdated boundaries but is encouraged to flourish.

Moreover, this book recognizes the impactful contributions of state and national leaders, consultants, and educational organizations. Their varied approaches, be it through community-based initiatives, consultancy support, or advocacy for legislative changes, collectively shape the education trajectory.

As we navigate the crossroads of education, it is evident that our system requires more than surface-level fixes. As we delve into the complexities of education at a pivotal juncture, it becomes clear that the system requires a united effort for profound change—the Ed. Matadores movement sincerely invites leaders at all levels—school, district, state, and national—to join us in revolutionizing education. Your unique experiences, insights, and innovative approaches are welcomed and vital as we collectively shape the future of learning. This book extends a heartfelt invitation to all leaders invested in students' future, urging them to join Matadores in revolutionizing the educational system.

Together, let us celebrate the diverse stories, break free from unnecessary and extreme constraints, and collectively pave the way for a brighter, more equitable and more innovative era in education.

Join the Ed. Matadores' movement today to become a driving force in the education transformation. We have a lot coming up the pike and we are just getting started.

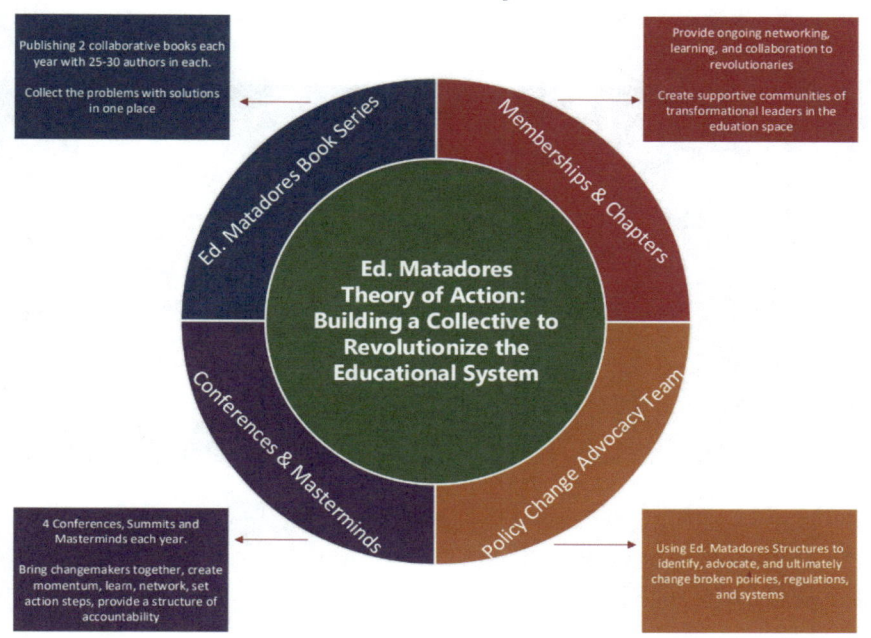

ED. Matadores Theory of Action

Ed. Matadores Theory of Action: Building a Collective to Revolutionize the Educational System

- **Ed. Matadores Book Series**: Publishing 2 collaborative books each year with 25-30 authors in each. Collect the problems with solutions in one place.
- **Memberships & Chapters**: Provide ongoing networking, learning, and collaboration to revolutionaries. Create supportive communities of transformational leaders in the eduation space.
- **Policy Change Advocacy Team**: Using Ed. Matadores Structures to identify, advocate, and ultimately change broken policies, regulations, and systems.
- **Conferences & Masterminds**: 4 Conferences, Summits and Masterminds each year. Bring changemakers together, create momentum, learn, network, set action steps, provide a structure of accountability.

Joining our movement is as simple as choosing one of three impactful avenues. First, consider inviting us to your district as speakers or consultants, where we can share insights and strategies for transformative change. Alternatively, contribute to our next book series by sharing your innovative stories and messages that can inspire the world. Finally, strengthen our collective impact by joining our community, where together, we can drive meaningful and transformative change in education. Your involvement in any of these ways is a crucial step toward building a stronger, more resilient educational future.

Connect via our social media:
- Join our FaceBook Group: Innovative Leaders Revolutionizing Education
  https://www.facebook.com/groups/6662385453872739
- Dr. Donna - https://www.linkedin.com/in/donnavallese
- Dr. B. - https://www.linkedin.com/in/drbglobal

Stay Informed:
https://inspiringleaders.network/

Invite Us to Your District:
https://forms.gle/GoJLYguTw5yq5ak18

Become an Author:

Schedule a Discovery Call with Dr. Donna:
https://calendly.com/inspiringleaders/discovery-call

References

ADKAR. *Nursing Management (Springhouse)*, *50*(4), 28–35. Amponsah, M., Haidar, E., & Staff Writers. (2023, May 20). *84% of admits accept spots in Harvard College class of 2027*. The Harvard Crimson. https://www.thecrimson.com/article/2023/5/20/class-of2027-yield-data/

Anderson, S.A. (1994). Synthesis of research on mastery learning. Information Analysis (ERIC Reproduction ED 382 567).

Arwood, E. (2011). *Language Function: An introduction to pragmatic assessment and intervention for higher order thinking and better literacy.* London and Philadelphia: Jessica Kingsley Publishers.

Arwood, E, Robb B, & Rostamizadeh A, (2018), *Learning to read and write, Neuro-Viconic Education System,* Apricot INC.

Arwood, E. (2011). *Language function: an introduction to pragmatic assessment and intervention for higher order thinking and better literacy.* Jessica Kingsley Publishers.

Arwood, E., Debreczeny, L. & Rostamizadeh, A. (2018), *Drawing Thinking, A supplement to the Neuro-Viconic Education System.* Apricot Inc.

Barbhuiya,Towfiqu. Unsplash. November 29, 2023. https://unsplash.com/photos/a-chalkboard-with-the-word-possible-written-on-it-Jxi526YIQgAutm_content=creditShareLink&utm_medium=referral&utm_source=unsplash

Barbour, M.K. The Shift to Distance Learning: Tracing the Roots of 100+ Years of Practice and Opportunity. *TechTrends* 65, 919–922 (2021). https://doi.org/10.1007/s11528-021-00670-0

Bloom, H. S., Unterman, R., Zhu, P., & Reardon, S. F. (2020).

Bridges, W. (1991, 2003, 2009, 2017) Managing Transitions, Da Capo

Bridges, W., & Bridge, S. (2017). *Managing Transitions: making the most of change.* London Nicholas Brealey Publishing.

Calagari, M. F., Sibley, R. E, & Turner, M.E. (2015) A roadmap for using Kotter's Organizational change model to build faculty engagement in accreditation. *Academy of Educational Leadership* Journal,19(3).29.

Can Pharm J (Ott). 2017 Apr 6;150(3):198-205. doi:10.1177/1715163517701470. PMID: 28507655; PMCID:PMC5415066.

Canada, G. (May 2013). *Our failing schools. Enough is Enough* [video]*!* TED Conferences.

https://www.ted.com/talks/geoffrey_canada_our_failing_schools_enough_is_enough

Cooper, J. D. (2006). *Literacy: helping children construct meaning* (6th ed. ed.). Boston: Houghton Mifflin Co.

Debreczeny, L. M. (2023). *Story Pictures: Draw, Write, Read*. Vancouver, WA: INSL LLC.

Della, C. (2017). Discourse of transformation in organizational change management. SHS Web Conf. 33 00039. DOI: 10.1051/shsconf/ 20173300039.

DeMatthews, D. (2015). Making sense of social justice leadership: A case study of a principal's experiences to create a more inclusive school. *Leadership and Policy in Schools, 14*(2), 1–28.

DeMatthews, D., & Mawhinney, H. (2014). Social justice leadership and inclusion: Exploring challenges in an urban district struggling to address inequities. *Educational Administration Quarterly, 50*(5), 844-881.

Edgar, D. W. (2012). Learning theories and historical events affecting instructional design in education. *SAGE Open,* https://10.1177/2158244012462707

Duby, P. (1981). Attributions and attributional change: Effects of a Mastery learning instructional approach. Paper presented at the Annual Meeting of the American Educational Research Association, Los Angeles, CA (ERIC Reproduction ED 200 640).

Durdella, C. & Durdella, N. (2009). Success Rates for Students Taking Compressed and Regular Length Developmental Courses in the Community College. Community College Journal of Research and Practice. 34. 39-54. 10.1080/10668920903385806.

Dweck, C. (2006). Mindset: The new psychology of success. New York, NY: Ballantine Books.

Gay, G. (2018). Culturally responsive teaching: Theory, research, and practice (3rd ed.). Teachers College Press.

Geltner, P. & Ruth, L. (2001). The Influence of Term Length on Student Success. Santa Monica College Office of Institutional Research.

Gray, P. (2013). *Free to learn: Why unleashing the instinct to play will make our children happier, more self-reliant, and better students for life.* Basic Books/Hachette Book Group.

Guerra, P. L., & Pazey, B. L. (2016). Transforming educational leadership preparation: Starting with ourselves. *The Qualitative Report, 21*(10), 1751.

Guskey, T., & Pigott, T. (1988). Research on group-based mastery learning programs: A meta-analysis. Journal of Educational Research, 81(4), 197-216.

Hernández, Eliezer, "The Identification and the Influence of Urban School Leaders' Personal Beliefs, Attitudes, and Behaviors on Leading Urban Social Justice Schools" (2020). *Education Doctoral.* Paper 439.

Holzweiss, P. C., Polnick, B., & Lunenburg, F. C. (2019). Online in half the Time: A Case Study with Online Compressed Courses. Innovative Higher Education, 44:299-315.

Jack, Anthony Abraham. (2019, March 1). *The Privileged Poor: How Elite Colleges Are Failing Disadvantaged Students.* Harvard University Press.

Khlaif, Z. N., Salha, S., & Kouraichi, B. (2021). Emergency remote learning during COVID-19 crisis: Students' engagement. *Education and information technologies, 26*(6), 7033–7055. https://doi.org/10.1007/s10639-021-10566-4

Knox, L. (2023, August 2). *The common app enters an uncommon era.* Inside Higher Ed. https://www.insidehighered.com/news/admissions/traditional-age/2023/08/02/colleges-change-essay-prompts-after-affirmative-action

Kouzes, J. M., & Posner, B. Z. (2012). *The leadership challenge* (6th ed.). San Francisco, CA: John Wiley & Sons.

Kulik, C., Kulik, J., & Bangert-Drowns, R. (1990). Effectiveness of mastery learning programs: A meta-analysis. Review of Educational Research, 60(2), 265-299.

Ladson-Billings, G. (2009). The Dreamkeepers: Successful teachers of African American children. John Wiley & Sons.

Leithwood, K., Louis, K. S., Anderson, S., & Wahlstrom, K. (2004). *How leadership influences student learning.* Retrieved from https://www.wallacefoundation.org/knowledge-center/Documents/How-Leadership-Influences-Student-Learning.pdf

Lessons from New York City's small schools of choice about high school features that promote graduation for disadvantaged students. Journal of Policy Analysis and Management, 39(3), 740-771.

Lifelong Books, an imprint of Perseus Books, LLC, a subsidiary of Hachette Book Group, Inc.

McDonald, T. (2017). School Closure and Loss: Guiding a District Through the Change Process. *Journal of Cases in Educational Leadership, 21*(2), 15–27.

Mezirow, J. (2003). Transformative learning as discourse. *Journal of Transformative Education, 1*(1), 58–63.

Mineo, L. (2020, April 8). *Time to fix American education with race-for-space resolve*. Https://News.Harvard.edu/Gazette. Retrieved August 31, 2023, From https://news.harvard.edu/gazette/story/2020/04/the-pandemics-impact-on-education/

Mitchell, G. (2015). *Bertnlannflys General Systems Theory*. http://www.minddevelopment.eu/systems.html.

Muccino, G. (Director). (2006). *The Pursuit of Happyness* [motion picture]. United States: Columbia Pictures.

Nair, P. (2020, April 8). *REBUILD SCHOOLS TO REINVENT EDUCATION An Open Letter to President Joe Biden, Education Secretary Miguel Cardona, and First Lady Dr. Jill Biden*. Https://Educationdesign.com/. Retrieved August 31, 2023, from https://educationdesign.com/rebuild-schools-to-reinvent-education/

National Center for Educational Statistics Fast Facts. (Retrieved 2023, November 22.) *Public and private school comparison*. https://nces.ed.gov/fastfacts/display.asp?id=55

Neitzel, M. (2022, November 15). *More than 80% of four-year colleges won't require standardized tests for fall 2023 admissions*. Forbes. https://www.forbes.com/sites/michaeltnietzel/2022/11/15/more-than-80-of-four-year-colleges-wont-require-standardized--tests-for-fall-2023-admissions/?sh=7219a1557fb9

Nelson, S. W., & Guerra, P. L. (2014). Educator beliefs and cultural knowledge: Implications for school improvement efforts. *Educational Administration Quarterly, 50*(1), 67-95.

Newell, C. (2018, July 18). *Change as an opportunity: A strategic approach to change management*. Forbes. Retrieved August 31, 2023, from https://www.forbes.com/sites/forbeshumanresourcescouncil/2018/07/20/change-as-an-opportunity-a-strategic-approach-to-change-management/?sh=3323996c2241

Newman, S., & Latifi, A. (2021). Vygotsky, education, and teacher education. *Null, 47*(1), 4-17. https://10.1080/02607476.2020.1831375

Northouse, P. G. (2018). *Leadership: Theory and practice*. Thousand Oaks, CA: Sage.

Pinder, P. (2017). Factors influencing career choices of Black, Latino, and White students: A synthesis of the literature. Journal of Career Development, 44(2), 87-104.

Raywid, M. A. (1998). Small schools: A reform that works. Educational leadership, 55(4), 34-39.

Saul, S. (2023, July 3). *Harvard's admissions is challenged for favoring children of alumni*. The New York Times.

https://www.nytimes.com/2023/07/03/us/harvard-alumni-children-affirmative-action.html

Shields, C. M. (2010). Transformative leadership: Working for equity in diverse contexts. *Educational Administration Quarterly, 46*(4), 558-589.

Shields, C. (2017). *Transformative Leadership in Education* (2nd ed.). Taylor and Francis. Retrieved from https://www.perlego.com/book/2193163/transformative-leadership-in-education-equitable-and-socially-just-change-in-an-uncertain-and-complex-world-pdf (Original work published 2017)

Skinner, B. F. (1953). *Science and human behavio*r: Simon and Schuster.

Skipper, J. (2019, July 19). *Flourishing during change: An alternative to fight or flight.* Change Management Review. Retrieved August 31, 2023, from https://www.changemanagementreview.com/flourishing-during-change-an-alternative-to-fight-or-flight/

Sleeter, C. E., & Grant, C. A. (1999). Making choices for multicultural education: Five approaches to race, class, and gender. John Wiley & Sons.

Slidebean.Unsplash. November 29, 2023. https://unsplash.com/photos/person-using-macbook-pro-on-brown-wooden-table-J3AV8F-B42Mutm_content=creditShareLink&utm_medium=referral&utm_source=unsplash

Smith, R. (2016). *Metamorphosis and the management of change.* Journal of Philosophy of Education, 50(01), 8-19. Doi:101111/1467-9752.12169.

Sohmen, V. S. (2016). Change management and theory U leadership. *International Journal Of Global Business, 9(2)*, 102–11 http://academic.regis.edu/spsugmod/capstone.htm.

Teixeira B, Gregory PAM, Austin Z. How are pharmacists in Ontario adapting to practice change? Results of a qualitative analysis using Kotter's change management model.

Theoharis, G. (2007). Social justice educational leaders and resistance: Toward a theory of social justice leadership. *Educational Administration Quarterly, 43*(2), 221–258.

UNESCO (2020). COVID-19 Education Response. Retrieved from: https://en.unesco.org/covid19/educationresponse/globalcoalitio

Van Tiem, D., Moseley, J. L., & Dessinger, J. C. (2012). Fundamentals of performance improvement: Optimizing results through people, processes, and organizations (3rd ed.). San Francisco, CA: Wiley/International Society for Performance Improvement.

Vygotsky, L. S. (1962). *Thought and language.* Cambridge, M.I.T. Press, Massachusetts Institute of Technology

Wong, Q., Lacombe, M., Keller, R., Joyce, T., & O'Malley, K. (2019). Leading change with

Wilson, F. R. (1998). *The hand.* New York: Vintage Books; A division of Random House, Inc.

Yoon E., Lubienski C., & Lee J. (2018). The geography of school choice in a city with growing inequality: The case of Vancouver. Journal of Education Policy, 33(2), 279–298.

Zaric, Marija. Unsplash. November 29, 2023, https://unsplash.com/photos/a-sign-that-reads-we-can-just-imagine-VlQLQtCJZr8utm_content=creditShareLink&utm_medium=referral&utm_source=unsplash

Made in United States
Troutdale, OR
12/12/2023